Dead Snails
Leave No Trails

DEAD SNAILS
LEAVE
NO TRAILS

Natural Pest Control for Home and Garden

by

Loren Nancarrow
& Janet Hogan Taylor

Ten Speed Press

Berkeley, California

1🖘

Ten Speed Press
P.O. Box 7123
Berkeley, California 94707

A Kirsty Melville Book

Distributed in Australia by E.J. Dwyer Pty. Ltd., in Canada by Publishers Group West, in New Zealand by Tandem Press, in South Africa by Real Books, in the United Kingdom and Europe by Airlift Books, and in Singapore and Malaysia by Berkeley Books.

Interior design by Victor Ichioka

Interior illustrations by Janet Hogan Taylor

Cover design by Fifth Street Design

Cover illustrations by Ellen Sasaki

Library of Congress Cataloging-in-Publication Data

Nancarrow, Loren.
    Dead snails leave no trails : natural pest control for home and garden / by Loren Nancarrow & Janet Hogan Taylor.
        p.   cm.
    "A Kirsty Melville book"—T.p. verso.
    Includes bibliographical references (p.   ) and index.
    ISBN 0-89815-852-4 (pbk.)
    1. Garden pests—Control. 2. Plants, protection of. 3. Household pests—Control. I. Taylor, Janet Hogan 1954- . II. Title
SB603.5.N36 1996   96-12460
635'.0496—dc20   CIP

First printing, 1996

Printed in Canada

    3 4 5 6 ‑ 00 99 98 97

CONTENTS

INTRODUCTION

When nature is left to her own rhythm, plants and animals flourish. Rarely does one life form grow to unmanageable numbers, unless humankind attempts to alter the balance. Unfortunately, in our efforts to harvest maximum amounts of food, we've come to view all insects as enemies. In order to deny a hungry biting pest a human meal, we've unleashed the full power of our technology. We have created chemical poisons to kill and chemical fertilizers to encourage growth. They each appear to achieve their objective, and in the case of chemical pesticides, they do their job too well. Most are indiscriminate and kill everything with which they come into contact. Too many of the victims are beneficial insects and animals, which pollinate, break down organic matter, and kill pests. They all die under the mist of poison.

In a yard or garden where chemical fertilizers are used, there is a shortage of beneficial earthworm activity, and the soil lacks organic matter. Things are green and growing, to be sure, but the balance is upset. When it rains, the chemical runoff poisons ground water and streams, rivers, and ultimately, the ocean.

In an organic garden, there are a few pests, but there is also an army of insects, arachnids and other arthropods, reptiles, mammals, and birds waiting to pounce. In an organic garden you'll witness the balance that nature intended. There may be a snake slithering underfoot, but it's working to keep rodents to a minimum. There may be insects flying about, but many are on patrol for a meal we'd be pleased for them to eat.

Who can resist stopping for a moment to watch a butterfly in flight? They are gentle and delicate creatures, landing on flowers, unfurling their proboscis, and then drinking nectar. Their colorful wings pump up and down as they feed, as though helping to draw in the sweet juices. Few people would purposely kill butterflies, and yet, when we spray poison indiscriminately, butterflies die in great numbers. Before you decide to kill the caterpillar that's chewing on your passion vine, consider that it could be the larva of a beautiful gulf fritillary, a prized butterfly. When people spray trees for aphids, they kill birds, and when they choose poisons to kill cabbage beetles, they may be killing the toad that's been helping around the garden as well.

We have chosen lifestyles free of most poisons. Our vegetable gardens are places where our children play freely—we don't have to worry that they'll come into contact with toxins. The fruit in our yards is there for the eating, with no washing required. During the mild Southern California winter, we often spend early mornings outdoors with our families, eating, laughing, and watching western fence lizards do the push-ups that are their means of communication. These carnivores will devour dozens of insects each day, and all they ask from us is a warm rock and fewer toxic residues in their habitat.

In this book, we have chosen to approach pest control by first encouraging a natural balance. Beyond that, we believe in using our knowledge of insect and animal behavior to work against pests. We hope you'll find our favorite methods to be fun and successful. We also hope that by learning about some of the creepy crawlers you find in your yard, you'll come to appreciate nature's magnificent balance.

PESTICIDE SAVVY

(Synthetic vs. Natural vs. Biological)

For as long as humankind has existed, insects have generally been regarded as pests. But to be a true "pest," an organism must do one of the following: damage crops, destroy products, transmit diseases, stand in the way of human interests or needs, or simply become annoying. To achieve the goal of eradicating pests, chemical pesticides have been developed to battle the invaders. (A pesticide is defined as any chemical that is intended to kill pests.) Pesticides can be man-made or derived from plants, and care must be taken with all of them. Many scientists believe that no insect pest species has ever been completely eradicated by the use of chemical pesticides, and, in some cases, pest species have become even more of a problem as a result of pesticide use.

Synthetic pesticides are man-made chemicals produced for the sole purpose of killing insect pests and other pests, such as weeds. These chemicals are produced in many forms for different applications. They can be sprayed or dusted on plants and animals, or made into pellets and gaseous forms for application to the soil. The two major groups of synthetic pesticides are chlorinated hydrocarbons (such as DDT) and organo-phosphates (such as Malathion).

Chlorinated hydrocarbon compounds date back to 1874 and have been under great scrutiny in recent years. These compounds were once thought to be miracle cures for many plant pest problems throughout the world. They were used widely to treat everything from lice in Italy (DDT was credited in halting a typhus epidemic carried by lice) to the common cockroach in U.S. homes. Problems arose from some of the residual effects of these compounds; for example, DDT has been linked to such problems as thinning of shells in some birds' eggs. Some of the target insects of these chemicals, such as cockroaches and flies, have even become resistant or immune to them.

Organo-phosphates are basically contact insecticides that were discovered in the course of poison gas research around the time of World War II. Some of these compounds are very toxic to humans and animals, as well as to insects. A real danger of many of these compounds is that they can be absorbed directly through the skin, besides the usual methods of contamination— breathing them in or eating them. Malathion is one of the most-used organo-phosphates because it has a very short residual effect in the environment and is also less toxic to non-pest animals. Many species of insects that are resistant to chlorinated hydrocarbon pesticides will be killed by Malathion. In any case, great care must be taken when using any pesticide. Always read the label carefully, and follow the directions for applying the pesticide correctly. It's wise to wear full protective clothing during application because nearly all pesticides are absorbed through the skin. The label will instruct you about what minimal protective clothing is required. Professionals often wear rubberized garments and respirators.

Natural controls are those things occurring physically in nature that help keep insect numbers in check. Such controls are found in every backyard and in all parts of the world. Some examples of natural controls are: weather conditions, rainfall levels, the amount of shade in an area, and geographic location. For example, if you live in Alaska, the temperature will keep many tropical insects from taking up residency in your backyard. A wide river might keep a hopping insect from getting to your garden, but it might also be a breeding ground for mosquitoes. People have little effect on natural controls, but in today's age of jets and cars, many an unwanted insect has found its way to a new home with human help.

Biological controls involve those living things that keep insect populations in check. Insect predators, including toads, frogs, moles, birds, and predatory insects, are a good example. Many naturally-occurring diseases, caused by viruses, fungi, and bacteria, also keep insect populations down. It is in this area of natural checks and balances where man has often upset the balance of beneficial and destructive insects.

A pest-management method called biocontrol allows the introduction or augmentation of predatory insects, parasites, or diseases to a pest area in order to reduce the population of a specific pest. This method works best on large one-crop parcels where there is generally one major pest. A good example of this would be the introduction of *vedalia*, an Australian ladybug beetle, to control cottony-cushion scale, a pest of citrus trees.

Some biological controls that are not so species-specific are gaining popularity among gardeners and farmers alike. One of these is a bacterium called *Bacillus thuringiensis*. It attacks many species of caterpillars, including tomato hornworms and gypsy moths. Biological controls generally do not completely eliminate a pest, but a natural balance will occur once the control agent becomes established. Biological controls will continue to control the target pest year after year, and may only occasionally need to be augmented. But keep in mind that biological controls do not work overnight. Predators and parasites take time to become established, and insect diseases and pathogens take time to spread and infect new victims. It's difficult to sit back and watch your garden being fed upon when you've just treated it with a biological control, but if you give the controls time to take hold, the rewards will be well worth it.

Back in the 1970s, eradicating pests with chemicals wasn't working well and serious questions were being raised concerning the environment. The term integrated pest management (IPM) was coined to describe a new practice of controlling pests in crops and gardens. IPM is basically a pest management strategy that looks at all aspects of pest management and comes up with a comprehensive analysis of the problem to produce the maximum crop yield and the minimum adverse effects to humans and the environment.

The first step in IPM is to choose healthy plants and give them the best growing conditions possible. Next, use all the available information about crop rotation, eliminating pest host plants, timed plantings, and timed harvests to reduce the severity of crop damage due to pests. After that, if an insect or disease does become a problem, the next step would be physically controlling the pest. Physical control involves hand-picking, traps, and barrier methods of control. If those controls fail, biological controls are added to the program. Finally, if all else fails, chemical controls are used as the last resort. Integrated pest management is based on the knowledge that some damage will occur —the secret of IPM is to know when to act on a problem pest. Many truly "organic" gardeners agree with this practice until chemical measures are used. IPM techniques are mainly common sense approaches, so it's likely that most people have used some form of integrated pest management in their own gardens at one time or another.

In reading the following chapters, you'll find many ideas for your own integrated pest management program. Tailor the program to your own specific problems and needs by observing your garden carefully to understand which insects are pests and which ones are beneficial. If you have questions concerning the identification of insects, start with your local nursery. Most experienced nursery personnel are well versed in entomology (the study of insects) and can identify most pests in your area.

PESTICIDE SAFETY

When all else has failed and you feel you must use a pesticide, the following suggestions will help you use the pesticide safely. Remember that even relatively non-toxic pesticides can cause problems if used improperly.

~ When choosing a pesticide, choose a product that is registered (government-approved) for your problem pest. Don't try to kill everything with a broad-spectrum pesticide. Be certain the product you choose is intended for the pest and pest life stage you are trying to control.

~ Always read the entire label and follow it exactly. Never add more of the chemical than the label calls for. The label is a legal document that tells you everything you need to know when using that product. It spells out exactly the characteristics of the pesticide and its proper use.

~ If you have children or pets, store the pesticides in a locked cabinet. Keep the telephone number of the nearest poison control center in the cabinet and by your phone. Never remove the label from the container or pour a chemical into another container that does not have the same chemical label attached to it. You will need this label to tell the doctor exactly what your child got into. Sometimes antidote information is given on the label.

~ Wear gloves when handling and mixing the pesticide, and remember that many pesticides can be absorbed through the skin. Always mix a pesticide in a well-ventilated area. The precautionary statement on the pesticide label usually gives important information on the hazards of the pesticide as well as the instructions for handling it. This statement also explains any toxicity to other organisms, such as bees or fish.

~ Buy only what you need for the current problem. Some products break down over time and you will not be treating your problem properly if you use a pesticide that has been stored for a long time.

~ Spot treatment is better for your environment than a full-scale assault. Use the pesticide on the smallest area possible, keeping in mind that many pesticides kill beneficial insects as well as harmful ones.

~ Apply the pesticide when the pest is most vulnerable. If you have to use a pesticide, it's best to do so when it will be most effective. For example, spraying caterpillars, which can't move quickly, will be more effective than trying to spray the flying adults.

~ Never apply a spray-type pesticide when it is windy. Most pesticide companies recommend not spraying when the wind is over five mph. Early morning spraying usually works best.

~ Never smoke, eat, or drink when applying pesticides, or allow anyone else to do so in the application area.

Reference sources for more information concerning pesticides:

Your local County Agriculture Department, Farm Bureau, or Agricultural (Cooperative) Extension Office
Check the government pages of your local telephone directory for phone numbers.

National Pesticide Telecommunications Network
(800) 858-PEST
This 24-hour telephone hotline is sponsored by the EPA and the Texas Tech University Health Sciences Center School of Medicine.

California Environmental Protection Agency
Department of Pesticide Regulation
Environmental Monitoring and Pest Management
555 Capitol Mall
Suite 525
Sacramento, CA 95814
(916) 445-3846

HOME PEST CONTROL

ANTS

You wake up one morning to find ants all over your kitchen counter. It seems they've taken over your entire home. Ants are very opportunistic, and no matter how clean your home seems to be, they'll keep coming back by the thousands. Don't worry—help is on the way.

Ant eradication ideas and recipes

To get rid of the ants you see, spray a commercial window cleaner on the ants and their trail. Any cleaner with ammonia (or pure citrus extract) will work, or you can make your own solution. It will kill the ants and break their trail (and clean your counters at the same time).

> **•Ammonia solution•**
>
> 1 pint water
>
> 1 tablespoon ammonia
>
> Mix and spray on counters and windows.

You can also combat ants by sending poison back to their nest with them. Our simple indoor ant bait is an effective method. The borax-corn syrup mixture can work wonders on ants that enjoy a sweet dinner. Grease ants, which love oily foods, will ignore it. If you find your ants are the grease-hungry kind, try the ant death bait recipe on page 20—just mix the dry ingredients with lard or shortening until the mixture is crumbly.

If you can, follow the ants back to their nest. Here, you can also use the ant death bait in dry form. Omit the water, and sprinkle a thin layer of the acid/sugar mixture evenly around the nest opening. (Don't make piles that dogs can lick up, as they love sugar.) The ants will carry the mixture into the nest and feed the colony with it, killing those that eat it. Repeat the sprinkling as long as you see ants.

Now that you have found the problem nest, here are a few more options:

~ Pour boiling water on the nest to kill the beasts. It won't kill all the ants at one time, but after a few repeated treatments it should really cut down on their numbers.

~ A strong chile solution poured into the nest will not only kill the ants but make the nest unlivable.

~ Sprinkle cornmeal around the ants' mound opening. The ants eat the dry cornmeal, which expands inside their bodies and kills them. (This is an old remedy my mother remembers.)

There are several ways to prevent ants from becoming a problem in the first place. Follow any ant trails to their entry point (such as holes in the wall or floor) and plug the holes. Try using mentholated rub around windows and screens that can't be permanently sealed to repel the ants. Make sure to test the rub on a small area to see if it will stain before applying it to the entire edge of the screen or window. Another trick to help keep ants away is to pour a dab of eucalyptus oil on a rag and wipe it in your cupboards.

Know your ant enemy

Ants are members of the wasp class of insects. There are more than 3500 species of ants living in nearly every habitat around the world. All of these ants are social and live in colonies called nests or mounds. The colony consists of a queen and female workers. When a nest gets overcrowded (some nests have over a million ants) the queen will produce winged males and females that go out and establish new nests.

Different species of ants, looking for different foods, can invade your home at the same time. The pale pharaoh ant searches for fatty foods, while the thief ant prefers protein foods. One of the worst invaders, the Argentine ant, has caused havoc since its introduction to this country from Brazil in 1891. It is partial to sweet foods, but it will eat just about anything!

Scent trails left behind by a scout ant provide a chemical connection between the nest and a food source, like your kitchen. The trail only lasts for a few minutes, but that's usually long enough for the ants to get from the nest to the food.

Scientists have demonstrated that ants are capable of individual learning and of passing on what they have learned. They have the ability to display memory and correct mistakes, which explains why they can be so hard to get rid of.

• Hot pepper solution •

Suntea jar or any large jar

2-4 sliced hot peppers (serrano, habanero, or jalapeño work well)

Put sliced peppers into the jar and fill with hot water. Let the mixture steep for at least 24 hours. Remove the peppers and pour the solution into the nest.

Serving size: one quart

Sure, *you* can say a lot with a kiss, but ants can say even more! They communicate by exchanging chemicals in their mouths.

COCKROACHES

For most people, nothing makes the skin crawl like the sight of cockroaches scurrying around the house. No matter how clean your house is, if you see one roach, you probably have a hundred. To make matters worse, you could have more than one species of cockroach infesting your home at the same time.

• Sweet roach bait •

1 part sugar

1 part baking soda

Mix sugar and baking soda. Put the mixture in jar lids and place them in your kitchen and/or garage, along walls and baseboards, under sinks, or wherever you've seen roaches.

Ridding your home of roaches

There are many commercial products available that target roaches, the most common of which are pesticide sprays or bait preparations. With a bit of knowledge of cockroach lifestyles and food preferences, you *can* outsmart the unstoppable roach! Most cockroaches love sweet foods. Use their sweet tooth against them to whip up sweet roach bait—a deadly dessert. When the roach eats the bait, its body fluids will turn to water, and the gas it produces will virtually explode the insect. This is a great bait if you have children or pets, as it is less toxic than most baits.

Cockroaches like to run in sheltered areas (like along baseboards), so make some sticky traps and place them in these areas. It's easy—just spray adhesive or smear Tanglefoot (if the adhesive is not strong enough for the big roaches) on one side of a four-inch-square piece of cardboard. (Tanglefoot, an extremely sticky product perfect for making traps, is available at garden supply stores.) Make several and experiment with the size. When the roaches run across the trap and get stuck, you simply throw them in the trash. You will need to keep children and pets away from these, especially if you use Tanglefoot, because the sticky substance is hard to remove from skin and hair.

There are a few cockroach species that prefer a less-sweet dinner. Try a sweet treat first and switch to a fatty bait if you continue to see roaches.

A favorite bait that both ants and roaches love is equal parts boric acid and sugar (see page 20). This bait can be used in many ways—see page 7 for more ideas on safely using this boric acid/sugar bait.

Baits containing boric acid can be harmful when consumed over time. Care should always be taken when using any bait to make sure that children and pets can't get to it and eat it. (See page 20 for more information on boric acid's toxicity.)

Roaches, public enemy number one

Cockroaches are members of the *Blattaria* suborder of insects and are easily recognized by their flattened oval shape. In North America there are about fifty known species. Cockroaches have been recorded on earth for 350 million years and some scientists speculate they will still be here long after most life on earth is gone.

Cockroaches, which hitchhiked to the U.S., are tropical insects that prefer warm climates. The roach is not known to transmit any specific disease to humans, but it is a major household pest whose nocturnal food-hunting habits have driven many a homeowner crazy. Some of the more common cockroach pests are the German cockroach, wood cockroach, Oriental cockroach, and American cockroach.

Female cockroaches reproduce using an egg capsule called an *ootheca*. The eggs are laid inside the capsule and are either carried around by the female or dropped. There can be hundreds of young roaches, which look like tiny adults, in each capsule.

• Fatty roach bait •

$1/2$ cup boric acid or borax

$1/8$ cup sugar

bacon drippings

Mix dry ingredients together with enough bacon drippings to form a paste. Add some flour if needed to form soft balls. Place marble-sized balls on wax paper wherever you see roaches. Extra caution should be taken to keep this away from pets and children. The bacon makes this bait especially attractive to dogs. Discard when dry. Store extra balls in freezer for later use.

You think you have a roach problem? Just imagine how much more daunting pest control would be if you had Madagascar hissing cockroaches, which are over four inches long. And this will make you feel even luckier: prehistoric roaches were over *six* inches in length.

Many chemicals have been developed to kill roaches, but these insects have a remarkable ability to become resistant to chemicals in a very short time. Cockroaches can also live for long periods of time without food. Roaches have been known to survive in vacant houses for years, with only wallpaper paste for nourishment. Though to many people cockroaches are simply repulsive, their survival skills are truly remarkable.

MICE AND RATS

You thought it couldn't happen to you—a rodent invasion. A rodent infestation is usually pretty obvious and often overwhelming. The first signs of a rodent most people see are the droppings they leave behind. In the garden, rats and mice will dig up seeds and generally make a mess.

A mouse in your house?

The first step in eliminating rodents from your property is to try to eliminate any food or shelter the rodents need. Sometimes your garden is the food source, so removing it isn't practical. In that case, you will have to concentrate your efforts on destroying the rodents' shelter. One way to do this is to plug any holes that they're using with coarse steel wool. Wait until night when the rodents are out foraging for food, and then plug the holes. This is usually a temporary measure (because steel wool left to the elements will rust away), but it is quick and will give you time to do proper repairs. Steel wool placed around pipes indoors will keep rodents from moving from room to room.

Never leave cat or dog food outside for rodents to find. They are smarter than they look and will take advantage of this easy food source.

Mice especially love hiding under mulches that drought-conscious gardeners use to keep water loss to a minimum, so if you need to use mulches, rake them often to keep the mice from making this area their home. Be aware that rats are especially fond of ivy ground cover.

Rats and mice are sensitive to certain smells. Spraying outdoor baseboards with a solution of ammonia and water will deter them. They also dislike the smells of daffodils, hyacinths, and scillia plants. Try planting some in trouble spots.

Keeping the rodents out of your garden is much more difficult. Solid barriers around your garden will help deter most rodents, but they usually find a way around or under such barriers. Burying a ¼-inch wire barrier at least six inches deep is a definite plus.

Building a better mousetrap

Most people feel baiting or trapping the rodents is the only way to really make a dent in the population. Everyone is familiar with the basic snap traps, and they are still used and preferred by many people. Peanut butter makes an excellent bait for a mouse snap trap.

KetchAll, a new trap used by many zoos, is based on the paddle wheel principle. It resembles an old-fashioned jack-in-the-box with a hole going through the base. You place the trap along a mouse path and when the mice run through the hole, they are caught in a holding chamber. It can catch many mice (up to twenty) alive, depending on how many times you wind the trap. However, you're then faced with the unpleasant job of disposing of the live mice. It's up to you to figure out how you want to get rid of them. (Animal control won't help you, but some pesticide companies will trap and take the mice away and kill them—for a fee. If you don't want to kill the rodents, your only choice is to drive them out into the country and drop them off in a field.) An important reminder here is to check live traps daily. Failure to do this will cause the forgotten mice to suffer a slow death by starvation.

Another trap that is much less kind is the glue board. The mice and rats run across it and get stuck to it. You have to decide how to kill the caught rodent and then throw the entire board away.

Poison baits are popular with some people because they are easy to use, and generally you don't have to dispose of the rodents afterwards. A homemade oatmeal-cement bait is effective —the rodents die because they can't digest the cement.

A new rodent bait uses vitamin D as the poisoning agent. Vitamin D can be harmful to rodents (as it can be to humans) if too much is taken. For this bait to kill the mice, they must continue to eat it until they build up a fatal calcium imbalance.

A rodent's world

Rats and mice are able to live in a variety of environments, and no place is safe from these invaders. Any place bigger than one-quarter inch can be a perfect home. Some of their favorite places are sewers, basements, stables, and burrows under rocks and buildings. Every zoo in the world has an ongoing fight with rodents. The lure of free food and lodging is just too much for the rodents to turn down.

Rats and mice are very prolific. Mice start breeding at about eight weeks of age and rats at about three months of age. Each can have litters four times a year, averaging eight to nine young per litter. Rodents cause major economic damage and can transmit infectious diseases such as plague and typhus to humans.

Most rats and mice are nocturnal and have favorite runs and paths along sides of buildings, baseboards, and fences. They also have excellent senses of hearing, taste, and smell, their eyesight being their poorest sense.

TERMITES

No other insects bring terror to the hearts of homeowners like termites. These small insects can skeletonize the wood in your home until it is barely standing. Repairs are usually costly and inconvenient. But how do you figure out if you have the little home wreckers—before it's too late?

Looking for the silent destroyers

Most people don't realize that they have termites until it's too late and they're looking at large repair bills. Just a little snooping can save your wallet and your house.

Start in your garage, which is generally the first place drywood termite signs will be noticed. Once a month, look around the floor of your garage for a sand-like substance. It is about the size of onion seeds or cracked pepper and is generally a mixture of rust and cream colors. If you have a small magnifying glass, look at this substance to see if each granule has six long grooves. This substance, called *frass*, is excreted by the termite and pushed out of an exit hole in the wood. The grooves are formed when the excrement passes from the termite's body.

If you find frass, look directly up for the exit hole, which will look like a nail hole. There may be one or more of them. You now have a place to start fighting the little creatures.

Be sure to check wooden patio covers and decks this way also. Outdoors, winds can blow away the frass quickly, so try the following trick: Hold a sheet of white paper under the section you want to check, and tap the wood with a rubber mallet or small hammer. You'll be able to see the frass as it falls onto the paper. Check carefully around corners and seams, which are termites' favorite places to enter the wood. Don't think you're safe because you have a redwood patio or deck—termites will attack redwood also.

If your house has a raised foundation, you'll need to get out your trusty flashlight to check for subterranean termites. These termites construct earthen tubes from the soil to the wood in your home. Check for these tubes along the inside and outside of your home's foundation. Also look for mud coming out between boards or along the foundation. A knife blade poked along your foundation or supporting studs will easily pierce an affected board. Extremely tunneled boards will sound hollow when tapped with a hammer.

Treatment options

Now that you've found the pests, it's time to figure out what kinds of treatments are available to you as a homeowner, and especially which treatments you can do yourself.

First, try to determine how extensive your infestation is. Is there only one board that is infested? Is it easy to get to? If there are more boards affected, do they show signs of weakness? Tap boards and watch for falling frass, look for exit holes, and check for the most serious sign: very hollow-sounding boards with easily exposed tunnels. Remember that termites chew through wood slowly, so finding evidence of their existence doesn't mean they will devour your home in a week. You have plenty of time to plan your attack.

If you don't trust yourself to determine how extensive your problem is, call one of the many termite companies that offer a free home inspection. This will also give you a good starting point and help you later in determining a treatment. Watching the inspector work will also help you do the job again yourself. Ask the inspector to show you what frass or earthen tubes look like, and, if frass is found, keep some for later comparison.

The diagnosis of termites used to mean all-out pesticide warfare against the insects. Some pesticides that were used routinely had a residual effect of up to twenty-five years. Luckily, homeowners today have numerous options, many of which do not rely on any pesticides.

One of the most effective methods of control for drywood termites is to just remove and replace infected boards. Often this is the easiest and cheapest method. When you remove a board, check the ends of the board carefully to see if the termites tunneled out of that board into the next. If no exit tunnels are found, your problem may be solved.

Termite companies have many new weapons in their arsenal against termites, like using microwave radiation, electricity, heat, and cold. Specially designed equipment shoots the radiation or electricity directly into the termites' nest, killing them. Another machine can heat wood to over 150 degrees, which kills the insects. Still another machine freezes the wood, destroying the termites. The amount and area of wood that needs to be treated and the conditions where you live may determine which of these methods would be perfect for your situation.

Pesticides are still used to combat termites. A few products can be purchased by the homeowner but many can only be obtained by professional termite exterminators. Unless you know exactly how to effectively spray for termites, it is best to leave large-area treatment to the professionals.

When only a few boards need to be treated, you can use a spot spray (labeled for use against ants and termites) that comes with a long flexible tube. Place the end of the tube over a termite exit hole, then start spraying until you see spray backing up into the tube or coming out another exit hole. Go to the next exit hole and spray again, continuing until no further exit holes are found. This spray works well on drywood and powder-post termites, since they are usually confined. You'll want to keep an eye on the treated area to make sure frass doesn't start appearing again.

If you discover you have subterranean termites, the earthen tube must be destroyed before treatment can begin. With these termites, both the wood and the soil must be treated. Subterranean termites eat your wood but always maintain some contact with the soil. Breaking this contact is essential for complete control over this type of termite.

Finally, if all else fails or the area to be treated is very large, the only option left might be to have your entire house fumigated. The good thing about this method is that it will also kill any roaches or ants that have made their home in your home. The bad news is that it kills any beneficial spiders in your home as well.

GARDEN PEST CONTROL

ANTS IN THE GARDEN

You may be distressed to find that the same little critters that have been plaguing you in your home are in your garden as well. It seems like they're everywhere, and they are—except the polar regions. What to do (besides move to Antarctica)?

Attacking the ant army

Because many species of ants look alike, you could have many different species living in your home and yard at the same time without even realizing it. Knowing what type of food the ants are after will help you determine what control method will work best. If ants attack your fruit trees, try this chile-vinegar spray. (Warning: some solutions—especially those containing oils and soaps—can burn delicate plants, causing the leaves to dry up and fall off. Before you use any new solution on a plant, test it first on one or two leaves. If those leaves still look healthy after a day or two, go ahead and do a full treatment.)

For ants elsewhere in the garden, try ant death bait, served in a jar lid or cut-down paper cup. Place the cups throughout your garden and yard where you know ants will

• **Chile-vinegar spray for fruit trees** •

4 jalapeños, habaneros, or other hot chiles, seeded and chopped

2 cloves garlic

1 $\frac{1}{2}$ quarts water

2 oz. beer (try using the rest of the bottle or can as snail bait)

$\frac{1}{2}$ cup vinegar

Mix chopped chiles, garlic, water, and beer. Cover and bring to a boil for 5 minutes, then let the mixture steep in the pot for 24 hours. Add the vinegar, strain well, and pour into a sprayer. Spray leaves (but not blossoms). Test first to check for burning.

find them. To protect dogs and other animals from getting into the cups, it may be necessary to put a cardboard box (weighed down with a heavy rock) over the cup. You can poke small holes into the base of the box with an ice pick to give ants easy access and keep pets from eating the poison. Note: Boric acid is a liver and kidney toxin which, over time, can make children and pets sick. A small one-time dose will most likely cause only an upset stomach; however, if you're in doubt, contact the poison control center in your area.

Ants: soil workers

Ants, as bothersome as they can be to people, do serve a function in nature. Besides being scavengers, ants are great soil mixers. Ants turn over tons of dirt building their nests, and are often called the "composters" of the insect world.

Besides working the soil, ants are scrupulously clean. They have a comb on the middle joint of each front leg they use to clean their bodies. Some birds will actually allow ants to crawl on their bodies to clean them of unwanted parasites.

When ants die, their fellow ants carry off the bodies to an ant morgue. While to humans this looks like a very difficult task, ants can lift fifty times their body weight without effort.

APHIDS

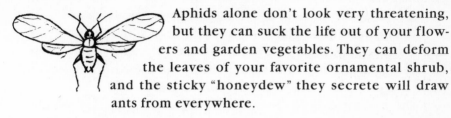

Aphids alone don't look very threatening, but they can suck the life out of your flowers and garden vegetables. They can deform the leaves of your favorite ornamental shrub, and the sticky "honeydew" they secrete will draw ants from everywhere.

Help is on the way

Luckily for you, there are numerous naturally-occurring aphid predators. The best known of these is the ladybird beetle or ladybug. Both the larval form (called aphid lions) and the adults prey upon aphids. Other predators include lacewings, syrphid fly larvae, and wasps. The adult forms of many of these predators only eat nectar and pollen, so you can encourage them by planting nectar-rich flowers and plants that produce a lot of pollen in and around your garden. Some good choices are daisies, mint, carrots, anise, and chives.

One ladybug can eat up to 5000 aphids in its lifetime.

A simple trimming or a strong spraying from the hose will sometimes do the trick to stop a small infestation of aphids. If somewhat stronger methods are needed, try one of the following.

To protect a desired vegetable, a sacrifice vegetable can be planted. If you know that the aphids in your garden love cabbage (and they usually do), plant some! The aphids will go for the cabbage and leave your other vegetables alone. This also makes the "seek and destroy" method of killing aphids much easier because they will be congregated in one spot.

However, if you want to grow cabbage and not give it to the aphids, try planting yellow and orange nasturtiums that will also attract the pesky aphids. They make an excellent garden border or companion planting. (Unfortunately, the nasturtiums may not look great with the aphids attacking them.) Nasturtiums planted around apple trees also work well at drawing the always unwanted woolly aphid away from the tree.

If you find that aphids are attacking your roses, mulch banana peels into the soil at the base of the rose bushes. This will strengthen them and ward off disease-bearing aphids.

Try spraying your plants with a mild soap solution, but keep in mind that some plants are easily burned by soap. Try your soap solution on a few leaves first and check them for burning—and don't forget to rinse the soap off after the treatment.

The new insecticidal soaps now available at garden supply stores kill aphids using fatty acids. They are very effective but must be used carefully and according to package directions.

Controlling the ants in your yard and garden can greatly reduce the aphid population (see page 19). Equal parts boric acid and sugar sprinkled in your garden will help. For complete recipes and more ant tips, see pages 19–20.

Aphids are attracted to anything yellow. Buy yellow sticky traps and place them in your garden, or make your own traps out of pieces of cardboard, yellow paint, and spray adhesive. Paint one side of the cardboard piece yellow. When it's dry, spray the adhesive on the painted side and place the traps in and around your garden. If that's too much trouble, a yellow plastic bucket filled with water and a bit of liquid soap will also work.

Commercially available insect growth regulators (IGRs) are artificial insect growth hormones that are sprayed on plants to target specific insect pests, such as aphids. They work by interfering with the insect's growth, development, or reproduction, stopping the life cycle of the pest. Many people are already familiar with IGRs in the new flea products, and these regulators are sure to increase in popularity as people become more aware of them. Ask for them at your local nursery.

Know your plant-sucking enemy

Aphids are one of the most economically destructive insects. They not only destroy crops and plants, but the money spent on pesticides to control them is astronomical.

Aphids, which are also called plant lice, are pear-shaped insects that suck the juices out of plant leaves, roots, and stems. They are characterized by two tube-like structures (cornicles) rising from the back of the abdomen. Aphids come in various sizes, but most are $\frac{1}{16}$ to $\frac{1}{8}$ inch long. They are usually green in color, but some species are brown, yellow, pink, or black.

Aphids have a complex life cycle. One of the most interesting aspects of their life cycle is that almost all the aphids you see in your yard are female. They reproduce without the need for male aphids and produce only wingless female offspring. This process, called parthenogenesis, goes on for several generations. Males and females with wings are only produced when it is time to lay eggs that need to overwinter.

Aphids produce honeydew, a sweet, sticky substance that ants love to eat. Some ants will actually tend the honeydew-producing aphids called ant cows. Not only will the ants harvest the honeydew for food, but they will protect and defend the aphids as well. Some species of aphids have become so dependent on the care of ants that without them they couldn't survive. A good example of this interdependence is the corn root aphid, which depends on ants to carry it from one corn root to another as the need arises. Here is where controlling ants in your yard or garden can greatly reduce the aphid population.

> It has been calculated that in 2.5 acres of crops there could be as many as 5 *trillion* aphids, which could produce 2 tons of honeydew a day.

Honeydew that dries on the plant appears shiny and can cause problems for a plant by becoming the medium for mold. Black mold, which has long been associated with aphids, can coat leaves and cut down on a plant's photosynthesis abilities. The aphid's role as a vector of disease is another major threat to plants. Just as the mosquito carries malaria from person to person, the winged form of the aphid carries diseases from plant to plant.

CUCUMBER BEETLES

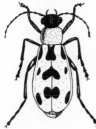
The leaves of your beautiful garden of cucumbers, melons, squashes, beans, peas, corn, beets, tomatoes, and potatoes are suddenly full of small holes. To make matters worse, now you are finding holes in some of your prized tree fruit and in flowers such as daisies and cosmos. Is it possible that the ¼-

to ⅓-inch beetles you're finding on the underside of leaves are doing all this damage? You bet!

Controlling the beetle

In large corn crops, farmers plow under all the old corn plants to deprive this hard-to-control beetle of shelter and thereby keep its numbers down. This is something all gardeners can do when each planting is finished producing. By removing all dead and finished plants and discarding or composting them, you remove the shelter needed by the adults to overwinter.

Planting early and late in the season can also help you avoid the beetles' peak season—the summer.

Another idea is to place a fine screen or small milk cartons over young seedlings. The beetles can destroy seedlings quickly, but most plants can tolerate the beetles' feeding once they're past the seedling stage.

Interplanting with such repellent plants as catnip, tansy, geraniums, and marigolds is known to help discourage the beetles. Radishes and nasturtiums are especially helpful.

Make beetle traps from open cans or milk cartons baited with garden targets, especially melon. Place these traps around your garden and check them early in the morning. (If you wait too long, the beetles will eat all the bait and leave before you have a chance to destroy them.)

If you have a strong stomach and a spare blender, you can also use the trap-caught beetles to prepare "cucumber beetle death repellent." Beetles don't like the smell of dead beetles in their feeding area, so this mixture should keep them away.

• Cucumber beetle death repellent •

50 (or more) cucumber beetles

2 cups water

Kill the beetles by placing them in a jar with a cotton ball soaked in fingernail polish remover. Put the dead beetles in a blender with the water and purée. Spray or drip the mixture, which should be fairly thin, around the plants in your garden.

Strength in numbers

The cucumber beetle has long been a garden pest, found on more than 200 kinds of weeds, grasses, and cultivated plants. This name is actually used for two beetles. The striped form (*Aclymmn vittata*) is yellow with three black stripes and a black head, and the spotted form (*Diabrotica undecimpunctata howardi* and a related Western species, *Diabrotica undecimpunctata undecimpunctata*) is greenish yellow with twelve black spots and a black head. The spotted cucumber beetle is also known by another name—corn rootworm—that describes the damage it does.

Both species have the same life cycle. The adults like to hibernate and spend the winter in old garden debris and around the bases of old plants. The adults emerge in early spring and lay their eggs at the base of host plants. After the eggs hatch, the larvae burrow into the soil looking for tender roots and underground parts of the stem. Here they can cause a lot of damage to gardens and crops, especially corn. The larvae continue to cause root damage until summer, when they pupate and emerge as new adults in July. Then the adults do their damage by chewing holes in the plant and transmitting viral and bacterial wilt diseases.

Very little is known about the natural predators of the cucumber beetle. There are a few natural predators, including tachinid flies, but they have little effect on the beetle population.

EARWIGS

Perhaps you've noticed bite marks on your flowers and the leaves of your beans, beets, corn, lettuce, strawberries, dahlias, or zinnias. After further inspection, you discover an earwig, a strange-looking insect with pincers on the end of its abdomen. These insects like to hide in dark places, but once you've found them you can stop the damage with a few simple strategies.

Bye-bye, earwig

In general, the earwig's natural predators (ants and yellow jacket wasps) do a pretty good job of keeping them in check. If you notice a lot of damage, it may be wise to import another predator. The tachinid fly, *Biganicheta spinipennis*, would be a good choice.

Traps are another very effective control method for earwigs. Several different methods rely on the same principle. Earwigs love to hide in dry, dark places, so place rolled-up newspapers in your garden before dark. Discard the newspapers the next day while the earwigs are still hiding in them. A six-inch piece of an old garden hose, either lying about the garden or stuck into the ground, will also make an excellent trap. Empty the traps each morning by shaking the earwigs from the hose pieces into a bucket of soapy water.

Bait traps are also very good for catching earwigs. Bury a small can flush with the ground and fill it partially with beer. Earwigs that are attracted to the beer will fall into the can and drown. This trap also catches snails, so if you have both pests, this is the trap for you.

You can protect your garden by spraying plants with a great earwig repellent made of garlic and soap. (It works on other unwanted insects as well.) Check for burning on all the plants in your garden before doing a full treatment.

Boric acid baits are also very effective for earwigs. Try the same one we recommend for ants (see page 20).

• Earwig repellent •

5 cloves garlic

1 cup water

3 drops liquid soap or detergent

Purée garlic and water in blender until liquefied. Strain the mixture and add 3 drops of soap. Add enough water to bring the mixture to one quart. Spray on plants.

Ear dwellers?

Earwigs are found throughout the United States and are easily spotted because of their large pincers. They are brown and about ½ to ¾ inch long, with a long segmented abdomen. They belong to the insect order *Dermaptera* (which describes their short leathery forewings), of which eighteen species are known to exist in the United States. The earwig probably got its name from people who feared that an ear was as good a place as any for this dark-dwelling creature to live. Even today, when we *know* earwigs don't live in ears, there are a few mysterious reports each year of people rushing to emergency rooms to have these creatures removed from their ears.

Most earwig species are nocturnal scavengers that feed on decaying plant matter, but the European earwig (*Forficula auricularia*) is a greenhouse pest. Some species are very beneficial and prey on aphids and small insect larvae. Garden damage due to earwigs is usually minimal.

The earwig overwinters in pairs. A male and female will hibernate together in cells in the soil or hollowed-out depressions under objects. In the spring the female lays her eggs and tends them until they hatch and leave the cell. Without careful cleaning of the eggs by the female, most eggs will become infected with fungus and fail to hatch. The earwig female is known as one of the true "mothers" of the insect world.

FRUIT FLIES

 You cut into a big juicy piece of fruit and find small white worms crawling inside. After checking more fruit from your trees, you discover much of the fruit has worms, and small golden flies seem to be hanging around your tree. This could be a *serious* problem.

An agricultural nightmare

In many states, fruit flies such as the Oriental fruit fly, Mexican fruit fly, melon fly, and Mediterranean fruit fly are categorized as "serious pests" requiring immediate intervention from state and/or county agricultural personnel. This usually involves the immediate sampling and surveying of fruit from host trees in the area to determine the infestation's severity. If the infestation is quite severe, stripping of all fruit from infected trees may be needed. And finally, a Malathion-laced bait may be sprayed on host plants to kill any remaining flies.

Recently another procedure has also been implemented—the release of thousands of sterile flies in the affected area. Fruit flies usually mate once, and if the ratio of sterile flies is very high, the chances of a nonsterile fly (called a wild fly) mating with a sterile fly will be good. You can tell a sterile fly from a nonsterile fly with a UV light. Sterile flies have a dye incorporated into their bodies during rearing. This dye will become visible under UV light. If you think you have a species of fruit fly infesting your fruit trees, call your local agricultural department for advice and an inspection.

However, it should be noted there are many kinds of fruit flies that are pests to gardeners but do not demand drastic action from agriculture officials. The cherry fruit fly is one such example.

Pepto Bismol to the rescue?

Many things have been tried to control fruit flies and most are marginally helpful at best. Basically you need to control them in the adult and pupal stages, because once the eggs are laid inside the fruit, it is difficult (or even impossible) to control the larvae without destroying the fruit.

New research has shown the dye in Pepto Bismol to be a very effective pesticide against fruit flies. It is hoped that soon the standard Malathion bait spray now used by agricultural departments will be replaced by a Pepto dye bait spray that will be completely harmless to humans and pets.

To fight fruit flies yourself, you can place sticky traps among the branches of trees. Put them out in early summer, when fruits are just starting to grow. You can purchase fruit fly traps from your local nursery or make your own. Some commercial traps contain a fly attractant that will make them much more effective.

Encourage predators by planting flowers that produce a lot of pollen (like daisies) around your trees. Many adult wasps eat pollen and use the fruit flies to continue their life cycle by parasitizing the fly larvae. The wasps lay their eggs on the fly larvae, and when the wasps hatch, they feed on the immature fly larvae, killing them.

The adult fruit fly, like the common house fly, has only spongy mouth parts, so it can't chew on your plants. You can use this knowledge against it by spraying a boric acid/sugar solution on your trees. The adult fly will be drawn to the sugar water on the leaves and get a lethal dose of boric acid in the process. Use the ant death bait recipe on page 20—just make sure to test a few leaves for burning first. This spray will also kill ants on the infested tree. This method works best when it is still wet, so early morning spraying is best. However, if your tree is prone to mold, use this spray only occasionally or wash it off after a few days.

The very tiny fruit flies that we've all seen hovering around ripe fruit can be controlled pretty easily in a small garden. Just take your hand-held vacuum cleaner out to the garden and suck them right out of the air.

The life of a fly

All fruit flies have a similar life cycle. The adults, which resemble small light brown houseflies with light and dark markings on their wings, lay their eggs inside developing fruit. One female may produce 800 eggs in her lifetime. The eggs hatch, and the white maggots, which grow to about ⅓ inch in length, feed inside the fruit. When the larvae are full-sized, they will leave the fruit and drop to the ground to pupate. The flies will stay in the pupal form in cool areas throughout the winter and the adults will emerge the following spring. However, in warm climates many generations of fruit flies can be produced throughout the year.

GREEN FIG BEETLES

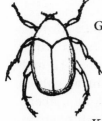

Giant green iridescent beetles are whizzing past your head and you discover they are heading for your prized grapevine or fruit tree.

Beating the beetles

Keeping your garden area clean of old plant clippings and prunings will help keep the beetle's population down by eliminating places where the beetle can lay its eggs. No beetle eggs in your yard means no adult beetles later.

Beetle larvae like the tender roots of lawns, and in heavy lawn infestations, soaking the lawn with soapy water will bring many of the grubs (or immature beetles) to the surface so you can pick them up and discard them. Many species of jaybirds love to eat the grubs and will wait patiently for you to expose them.

In areas under trees and vines where you know there are beetle grubs, you can use clear plastic sheeting to catch many emerging adults. Place the plastic sheeting under the trees in late spring, and seal the edges with two-by-fours weighed down with rocks or bricks. Tape sheeting around tree trunks to seal around the trunks. When the beetle adults begin to hatch from their pupal cells, you will be able to see them at the soil surface through the clear plastic. Now you'll be able to capture many adults before they mate and produce more grubs. The adults aren't very fast and can be picked up easily when one edge of the sheeting is rolled back. Dispose of the adults by dropping them into a bucket of soapy water.

Bait buckets can be placed near trees or gardens to lure the adult beetles. Fill a large bucket half-full of water, add malt extract and molasses, and allow it to ferment. The beetles will go after the bait, fall in the bucket, and drown.

Many people who have compost piles actually find the beetle grubs to be very beneficial. The grubs aerate the pile and move a lot of decaying material through their bodies, turning it into usable compost. However, care must be taken to remove these grubs in early summer before they reach adulthood.

A beetle of many names

Green fig beetles, also called green june or fruit beetles (*Cotinis nitida*), are most common in warm climates of the United States. The adults are about 1 inch long and very thick-bodied. Though the adults are known to eat the leaves and fruit of many garden plants, their favorites are peaches, nectarines, apricots, pears, apples, figs, grapes, melons, and tomatoes. The large white larvae are also pests, causing serious damage to the roots of lawn grasses and many ornamental and vegetable plants.

Green fig beetles pass the winter in the larval stage, feeding on roots deep in the soil. By mid-spring, the grubs reach full size and dig a cell in the soil. This is where the larvae will spend their pupal stage. In July and August the new adults will emerge to feed on fruit and foliage.

The eggs of the beetle are laid in dead vegetable matter, which the new larvae will feed on until winter, when they go underground. Keeping your garden clean will deprive this beetle species of a place to grow.

GYPSY MOTHS

 The trees in your yard betray the telltale signs of a gypsy moth invasion: what was once a beautiful tree has been reduced to bare limbs in a few days' time. It may be too late for that tree, but there is help for the trees that still have leaves left on them.

Go on the attack

The gypsy moth was accidentally released in 1869 by a naturalist who was interested in using it to develop a disease-resistant silkworm, and it has since defoliated millions of acres of trees in the eastern part of the United States. If you live in an area that has gypsy moths, you should plan your attack on this pest early in the spring. Controlling the population is an essential tactic in keeping the damage to a minimum. Gardeners in the West, where the gypsy moth is not established, should also be on the lookout for this very destructive insect and report any suspected gypsy moths to their local agricultural officials.

The first step in controlling this moth is to remove all egg masses from trees, outdoor furniture, and buildings. Each egg mass (1 ½ inches long and ¾ inch wide) contains up to 1,000 eggs and is covered with buff-colored hairs from the abdomen of the female. The eggs are laid in the summer months between July and September and should be destroyed on sight.

The larvae, which are quite distinctive, hatch in the spring and begin eating and doing damage to many species of trees immediately. If the egg mass was not laid on a tree trunk, the caterpillar will search for the nearest tree victim. Tree species that the caterpillars love are alder, apple, aspen, basswood, birch, hawthorn, oak, and willow. The caterpillar will also attack beech, blackgum, cherry, hemlock, hickory, hornbeam, larch, maple, pine, sassafras, and spruce if their favorite trees are not available. A burlap band placed around tree trunks can catch many caterpillars trying to go up into the tree to feed.

To use burlap banding: take a wide (two feet or so) piece of burlap and tape it on the tree trunk about two feet up. The burlap must go all the way around the tree, with a bit of extra for an overlap. Tie a string or cord around the middle of the burlap. Remove the tape from the burlap and fold the upper portion down over the cord and lower portion. This is now a caterpillar trap! When the caterpillars try to climb up into the tree they will get caught in the fold of the burlap. Check and remove caterpillars daily. Bands can also be made of sticky material, by placing a sticky substance (such as Tanglefoot) around the tree trunks. These bands are messier to use, but they work in much the same way as the burlap band and do not require daily checking.

Unfortunately, there are only a few natural enemies of the gypsy moth here in the United States. Its best-known enemies are the wasps *Hyposoter fugitivus* and *Apanteles schizurae*. The females of these wasps attack the caterpillars and lay their eggs in them. The eggs of the wasps then hatch and feed on the caterpillar from the inside, eventually killing it. To encourage these wasps, plant flowering plants that produce lots of nectar.

Other predators of the gypsy moth are the trichogramma wasp, which attacks the eggs of the moth, and spined soldier bugs, which will also attack the moth itself. Scientists are still studying many natural European enemies of the gypsy moth for application here in the United States.

In recent years, controlling the gypsy moth has been made easier with the use of the bacterium *Bacillus thuringiensis*, or *Bt*. Spray *Bt* as soon as you see any caterpillars. It is very effective, but it takes a few days to do its work. Pheromone traps for adults, which reduce the numbers of breeding moths, are also commercially available. The traps use a sex attractant to lure the moth into the trap, where a sticky substance immobilizes it.

A new method on the horizon is the fungus *Entomophaga maimaiga*, which has shown great promise in Virginia research trials. It was introduced into that state a few years ago, after it was identified in gypsy moth populations in New England in 1989. This year Virginia officials announced that in some counties they were able to cut back on pesticide spraying as a result of the fungus' effectiveness.

> A mature gypsy moth caterpillar can eat the equivalent of a square foot of leaves in one night.

The life of a gypsy

The gypsy moth (*Lymantria dispar*) is a member of the tussock moth family, and earned its name by being a notorious hitch-hiker. Unwitting humans transport the egg masses that the moths lay in trailer hitches, lawn furniture, and wheel wells. The gypsy moth and its relatives are serious pests of forest and shade trees.

The adult moths do not feed—their sole purpose is to mate and lay eggs. The eggs are laid by the female moth, which looks different from the male. The female is white with darker tan to brown inverted "V" markings on her wings. She has a wingspan of about 2 inches and is a poor flyer, if she flies at all. The male, which is smaller than the female, is dark brown in color with a black wavy pattern on its wings.

It is during its caterpillar stage that the gypsy moth causes all the damage. When the eggs hatch, the small caterpillars spin silken threads on which they can sail through the air by catching the wind. The caterpillars are easy to identify by the rows of blue and red dots on their backs. The first five rows of paired dots are blue, and the next six rows are red. Each caterpillar also has tufts of hair coming from its sides.

When the caterpillars reach full size, about 2 inches in length, they will form into pupae in the cracks and crevices of their host tree. The adults will soon emerge to start the cycle all over again. Luckily, the gypsy moth has only one generation per year.

HARLEQUIN BUGS

 At first glance, you think you see large ladybird beetles crawling on your prized cabbage. But wait, they aren't ladybird beetles—they're colorful stink bugs with black and orange markings. The beautiful harlequin bug isn't a beneficial addition to your garden at all—it's after your cabbage.

Harlequins don't clown around

The strikingly-colored harlequin bug (sometimes called the cabbage bug, calico bug, or fire bug) is definitely destructive to cabbage and other cruciferous crops in your garden. Yellowish patches on the plant's leaves, caused by the insect's feeding, are generally the first signs of damage you'll notice. In heavy infestations, the entire plant can be sucked dry and die.

Before planting your first seedling in the spring, you should be thinking of how to keep this pest in check before its population can build up. Harlequin bugs like plenty of ground cover in which to breed and lay their eggs. A clean and neat garden will go a long way in keeping the population down. However, no matter how clean your garden is, if you live next to an open weedy field or have a neighbor whose yard is a jungle, then you may have harlequin bugs. Harlequin bugs love mustard, so concentrate your efforts on eliminating this weed early.

Trapping may be a good next step to try if harlequin bugs persist in your garden. A trap crop also works well with these insects. Since they like cabbage and mustard, plant some just for them. Unlike aphids, harlequin bugs are fast runners, and if you pull the plant up to rid yourself of these bugs, you may actually spread them around. It is wise to first spray the bugs on the plant with a strong insecticidal soap and then remove the plant when the bugs are stunned. Dunking the plant in soapy water right after pulling it will ensure that all the bugs are dead before you dispose of the plant.

The parasitic wasp (*Telenomus*) is an important natural predator of the harlequin bug. Its primary target is the eggs of the bug. There is also a species of parasitic fly in the *Tachinidae* family that attacks the harlequin's eggs and nymphs.

You can also reduce the population of harlequins by hand-picking egg masses when you see them on leaves. The eggs are easy to identify—they are packed neatly together and resemble tiny white barrels with black bands around them.

A harlequin's life

The harlequin bug (*Murgantia histrionica*) is a member of the true bug order, *Hemiptera*. Unlike other insects we call bugs, only the members of this order should really be called "bugs." True bugs all possess a first pair of wings that fold flat over the back of the insect. The word *Hemiptera* actually means "half wing." These wings, called *hemelytra*, are usually leathery toward the base and membranous at the end and resemble a shield held on the back. True bugs also have sucking mouth parts, called beaks, that they use to pierce plants. Some species, like the harlequin's cousin, the bedbug, also use the beak to pierce human skin.

Adult harlequin bugs overwinter in plant debris and emerge in the spring to lay their unique barrel-shaped eggs. The eggs are usually laid on leaf surfaces, in clusters of at least ten. The eggs hatch into nymphs that look like miniature adults and can disperse rapidly to feed on desired plants. Both the adults and the nymphs are pests to the gardener.

JAPANESE BEETLES

You've just put in a new lawn, and you're ready for that first backyard barbecue, but suddenly you see brown patches appearing in your grass. Closer inspection shows small white grubs chewing on the roots of your lawn. White grubs can signify many kinds of beetles, so how do you know if your yard is infested with Japanese beetles? If it's May or later, look around your yard for the telltale damage of the adults. Leaves of shrubs and plants that have been chewed will look like lacy skeletons, and you may also see some small, metallic green and copper beetles, with six white tufts on the sides of their bodies, feeding on your fruit.

Crashing their lawn party

The best defense against the Japanese beetle is a good offense, so targeting the larvae early will achieve good results. In the past, broad-spectrum insecticides were poured on lawns in an effort to control this pest. A breakthrough in controlling Japanese beetles without harsh chemicals came when milky spore disease was discovered. This disease is caused by a bacterium (*Bacillus popilliae*) which, when applied to lawns and around trees and shrubs, effectively kills the immature larvae. Unlike insecticides, the milky spore disease kills the grubs without hurting earthworms, beneficial soil-dwelling organisms, or natural enemies of the beetle larvae that live in the soil. It is recommended that yearly treatment be established to provide long-term control for this pest.

Success has also been found with the release of parasitic nematodes. Two that have been particularly effective are *Steinernema glaseri* and *Heterorhabditis bacteriophora*. These nematodes work best when applied to warm, moist soils, and may not be as effective in early spring control. Most nurseries recommend applying nematodes in late spring or early summer.

Once the adult beetles emerge, your strategy needs to change. Commercial traps are available that use the female's pheromone or sex attractant to lure the males. These traps are useful in determining if you have Japanese beetles in your yard or how bad your infestation is. It is best to place traps away from your prized plants, since the trap will attract the beetles.

If you determine that you do indeed have the dreaded beetles, a simple and effective control measure is to dislodge and drown them. Early in the morning, when the beetles aren't very active, knock them from shrubs and branches onto a sheet and dump them in a bucket of soapy water. This process is time-consuming, but if done daily during peak infestations, it can provide a good measure of control.

A great natural enemy of the Japanese beetle is the tachinid fly (*Hyperecteina aldrichi*). If you have the pest beetle, then you probably already have the fly and you don't need to do anything special to attract it. The tachinid is sensitive to pesticide spraying, however, so avoiding pesticide use can prevent a decline in this helpful fly's numbers.

The beauty is a beast

Japanese beetles (*Popillia japonica*) have long been a pest in the northeastern part of the United States. These striking scarab beetles are about ½ inch long, with stout bodies of metallic green. Their wing covers (elytra) are coppery in color, and they have white tufts of hair sticking out along their sides. So far, efforts to keep this pest from establishing itself in the West have been successful, and agriculture officials are ever on the alert for it.

The Japanese beetle larva causes most of its damage by feeding on the roots of grasses and tender plants. Since the larvae live underground, treatment is difficult. Most of the time you can find the grub living about two inches below the soil surface. The grub stage occupies most of the life cycle of the beetle, with the adult beetle emerging from the ground around May or June.

Adult Japanese beetles like to congregate on plants and trees to feed and find a mate. They can cause damage to many types of trees, vines, and bushes, including apple, black walnut, American chestnut, elm, grape, and rose, and they'll also feed on mature tree fruit, leaving it unsightly. After mating, the adult female will lay her eggs back in the soil, leaving the eggs to spend the winter underground and hatch in the spring to begin the cycle again.

MEALYBUGS AND SCALE INSECTS

Little barnacle-like bumps about ⅙ to ¼ inch long are appearing on your citrus trees. Your neighbor has also found other bumps on his apples, figs, grapes, pears, and some ornamental shrubs. Though it may appear to be a plant disease of some kind, most likely you are looking at an insect pest, probably mealybugs or scale insects (which suck the juices right out of your plants).

Getting rid of the little suckers

Dislodging the insects from their host plants is quite an effective control. A strong spray with the hose will remove a great number of the pests. On small infestations, try touching a cotton swab dipped in alcohol to the insect, which should die in a few days. On larger infestations, wiping the insects with a rag saturated in alcohol will also work—just be careful not to burn your plants with the alcohol. You can also use oils to suffocate the insects, especially scales—try dormant oils in the winter, and, in the summer, special oils that won't burn the leaves. Check at your local nursery for the best oil to use.

Many parasitic wasps, lacewings, hover flies, and ladybird beetles are natural enemies of the mealybug and scale. The vedalia ladybird beetle (*Rodolia cardinalis*) preys on cottony-cushion scale, a serious pest of citrus trees. A beetle appropriately named the mealybug destroyer (*Cryptolaemus montrouzieri*) has been introduced in many areas to control these insects. Check with your local nursery to see if the purchase of these predators would be beneficial in your area.

Controlling ants is very important in controlling mealybugs. Just as with aphids, ants will defend mealybugs from predators and use the honeydew they produce for food. See page 19 for information on controlling ants.

Stuck for life

Mealybugs and scales are closely related and are both members of the insect family *Coccidae*. The armored appearance of these insects is caused by the waxy material they exude as a covering for their entire body. They do damage to plants by inserting their mouth parts into a plant and sucking out the plant's juices.

Their ability to harm great numbers of plants is a result of the large numbers of young they can produce. It has been estimated that one female of this family can produce up to thirty million young in one year!

In general, both mealybugs and scales have very similar life cycles. Females produce a waxy egg sac, and, in some species, give birth to live young. In some species the egg sac is deposited on a stem, and in some others the female carries the eggs under her shell until they hatch. Newly hatched nymphs have legs, but once they begin feeding on a plant, they start to secrete their covering. Scale insects become fixed to the plant at that spot, but some mealybugs can still move about, although they're quite sluggish. The females remain in this fixed state their entire lives. The males, when they're nearly grown, form into an active, two-winged insect that looks like a tiny fly. At that stage, the male is incapable of feeding and his sole job is to mate with a female.

MOSQUITOES

You can hear them coming; they're like bombers on a desperate mission. Their sneak attacks are sometimes so good they've come and gone before you notice they've attacked you. But the bites they leave behind will remind you for days that they've achieved their mission: extracting your blood in order to complete their reproductive cycle.

Grounding the bombers

There are many strategies for repelling mosquitoes and preventing them from lighting on you and biting. There are a number of commercially available products which can be quite effective when used properly. In addition, citronella candles can provide protection from mosquitoes, but only for a limited distance around the candle. The problem here is that you can't carry a candle with you everywhere you go.

Citrosa geraniums planted around your yard can help repel mosquitoes, but in areas of heavy infestations the geraniums alone may not be enough. For indoor mosquito protection, try growing the geraniums indoors—or even bringing in a bouquet from outside. Many other plants and herbs are known to repel mosquitoes. Some plants, such as eucalyptus, mint, and rosemary, not only give protection from mosquitoes, but also from fleas, ticks, and gnats. Rubbing the herbs directly on the skin provides the best protection. Start an herb garden and let it do double duty—herbs that are good in cooking can, when planted in hanging baskets near doors and windows, help keep pesky

> To help stop the itch of a mosquito bite, mix a paste of equal parts of baking soda and water and apply to the bite.

mosquitoes out of your house. Some good choices besides the ones mentioned above are basil, lavender, sage, and thyme.

Mosquito fish (*Gambusia affinis*), which eat mosquito larvae, can be added to ponds to keep mosquitoes in check. In some areas you can obtain the fish directly from your county agriculture department.

They want to suck your blood

Only the female mosquito bites its victims for blood, in order to complete her reproductive cycle and lay eggs. It is when the mosquito bites her victim that she really becomes a danger to humans, because her saliva can carry many harmful diseases, including malaria, dengue fever, and filariasis, just to name a few. Fortunately, there are few mosquito-borne diseases reported in the United States each year.

Mosquitoes must have water in which to lay their eggs, so draining any standing water you find around your yard will go a long way toward reducing the mosquito population. (An old rain-filled flower pot that you've forgotten about can provide the perfect habitat for hundreds of mosquito larvae.) Some people who have ornamental water ponds may wish to float a thin layer of mineral oil on the surface of the pond to keep out mosquitoes. This works by cutting off the oxygen to the breathing tube of the larvae, killing them. Before using this oil film, make sure that it won't hurt your fish.

ROSE MILDEW

You love your beautifully cool coastal weather, but the night and morning low clouds that are so great for your strawberries are causing a horrible mildew problem on your roses. What can you do?

A mildew solution

There are several simple fixes for rose mildew. It's best to combat the mildew before it starts by mixing up our low-pH baking soda-and-water rose mildew solution. You can also try spraying clear water on your plants early in the morning, to knock off the spores responsible for the mildew. After mildew (or rust) has appeared, try using our stronger rust and mildew solution, which contains horticultural oil and kelp extract.

• Rose mildew solution •

2 tablespoons baking soda

1 gallon water

1 teaspoon of commercial sticker/spreader (available at garden shops, or substitute 1 teaspoon liquid Turtle Wax)

Mix together and spray on your roses.

• Rust and mildew solution •

2 tablespoons baking soda

1 gallon water

6 tablespoons horticultural oil

2 tablespoons kelp extract

Mix together and spray on your roses when rust and mildew appear.

SNAILS AND SLUGS

The telltale slime trails are appearing in your yard, and you're finding round holes in some of your favorite plants and shrubs. There's no hiding it—snails and slugs (or both) have found a home in your yard.

Dead snails leave no trails

Snails and slugs can be effectively controlled in your garden or yard by several different methods.

~ Ring plants that snails and slugs love, such as strawberries, with a thick layer of bran. (Yes, bran!) It can be bought at any feed store (or grocery store, though it will cost more there), and works great to control snails and slugs. Besides being inexpensive, it is completely harmless to children, pets, and other animals. Diatomaceous earth can also be spread around plants to control snails. When a snail or slug crosses the diatomaceous earth, the silica in the earth cuts the body of the snail or slug and kills it. If you live in an area where sawdust is available, it works in much the same way diatomaceous earth does. Unfortunately, all these must be reapplied after a rain or heavy watering.

~ One tried-and-true remedy is the old-fashioned beer trap. Place a saucer of beer (with the lip at ground level) in your yard or garden in the evening, and collect the little beer-lovers in the morning. Dispose of them in a bucket of salty water or give them to the ducks at your local pond; ducks love snails and will find them a treat! A yard with a duck will not have snails or slugs.

~ Small children love to collect snails. You'll be surprised how fast the snails will disappear if you offer a penny per snail!

~ Traps made out of small cans can also reduce the snail population. Bury the can almost to its rim and place a piece of decaying fruit at the bottom. Check and empty the can daily. (You may catch more than snails with this method.)

~ Many gardeners, if they have a light infestation of snails, like hand-picking for control. Hand-picking works best just after a rain at dusk, using a strong flashlight.

~ Slugs and snails love to hide under things in the daytime. Use this knowledge to trap unwanted slugs with old flower pots. Place a few old flower pots, upside down and with the drain holes covered, in the areas where you know slugs live. Leave a crack between the ground and the pot, so the slugs can get under the pot. Check daily for hiding slugs and dispose of them.

~ A small border of copper stripping can effectively keep slugs and snails out of your garden, as they will not cross copper. Tack stripping along the edge of a raised bed frame or around tree trunks. Several commercial copper products are available at your local nursery for this purpose. If you live in an area where the giant "banana" slugs live, then slug control takes on a new meaning for you. Some of these giants can be 6 inches or more in length. The copper method works well for keeping banana slugs out.

~ Much has been written lately on the benefits of purchasing decollate snails (*Rumina decollata*) to control the brown garden snail. Yes, these predaceous snails do eat many brown garden snails, and in the citrus orchards of Southern California they have provided excellent control of the brown garden snails without pesticides. But what do they eat when all the garden snails are gone? In gardens, the decollate snail will also feed on small plants, seedlings, and flowers when their favorite prey is not available. Also, decollate snails are not allowed in some areas of the United States. Check to see if they are allowed in your area before purchasing them, and keep in mind that they may attack your plants after they've taken care of your brown snail problem.

Moving through life slowly

Snails and slugs are both members of the class of invertebrates known as mollusks. The mollusk class has over 80,000 species worldwide that live both on land and in water. Most people find snails and slugs pretty disgusting, but they have a few cousins, including clams, oysters, and abalones, that are much-desired food sources for humans.

Slugs are basically snails without shells. Both move on one muscular foot on mucus slime trails. This mucus dries and leaves the silvery trails with which we're all familiar.

Snails and slugs feed on decaying matter and fresh plants. They do most of their damage to young seedlings and low-growing fruits, such as strawberries. In an orchard, snails and slugs would be of some benefit if they ate only the fallen rotting fruit, but they will climb a tree for fresh fruit as well.

SOW BUGS

Most people have seen small sow bugs (also called pill bugs), which like to hide in dark, damp places, and haven't thought much about them. However, if you decide to plant strawberries in your garden, you may soon be quite aware of the damage these critters can cause.

Sending sows south

Sow bugs need a moist environment of damp, decaying plant material in order to live. Keeping your garden clean of dead leaves and being water wise will go a long way toward reducing the population of sowbugs. Not letting fruits and vegetables touch the ground will also help prevent damage from these ground dwellers. Placing vegetables on top of strawberry baskets is a good way to keep them off the ground while allowing air to circulate around them.

Strawberries are a favorite target for sow bugs. These low-growing plants provide everything a sow bug could want. The leaves of most strawberries lay directly on the ground, keeping the soil moist underneath. Of course the fruit is a great prize, especially if it is overripe. Any method you can use to raise the plants up a bit will help, but this isn't always possible with strawberries. Prune any old leaves immediately and use small rocks to keep the fruit off the ground.

Spread diatomaceous earth (preferably food grade) around the plants, ¼ inch deep and 2 inches wide. The sow bugs that try to cross the diatomaceous earth will pick up particles of earth, which will cut into their exoskeletons and eventually kill them. (This method works best on slugs and snails, which do not have exoskeletons. Keep in mind that by controlling slugs and snails, you can determine what damage, if any, the sow bugs are causing.)

Make a sow bug trap with an old flower pot. Turn the pot upside down in an area where you know there are sow bugs. Now lift up one side about ½ inch by resting it on a small rock. The sow bugs will be attracted to the dark place and you can dispose of the ones you catch in a bucket of soapy water in the morning. Black plastic placed on the soil around your plants will also deter sow bugs by making the soil too hot for them.

Land lobsters

Yes, that's right—sow bugs are related to lobsters and crayfish. They are land dwelling crustaceans, not insects. Sow bugs have segmented body coverings that resemble shells. Most sow bugs are about ½ inch long and have seven pairs of legs. They also breathe through gills, which is why they must have a moist habitat. Overall, sow bugs are beneficial to the environment. They play an important role in recycling organic matter, are often found feeding on decaying fruit, and will generally choose decaying plant matter over fresh.

> Ever seen a bright blue sow bug? These unusual critters aren't a different species—they just happen to carry a harmless nematode that makes them turn blue. Scientists still don't know why. Yet another mystery of the animal kingdom...

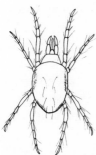

SPIDER MITES

You see small dots moving on some of your plants. Closer inspection reveals minute "spider" webs and tiny light specks on some leaves. You're sure these weren't there a few days ago—it looks like a mite attack.

More mites make right

For particularly bad infestations of spider mites, you may want to release commercially available predatory mites. This can be a very useful method for control because these mites feed only on other mites—they don't eat plants. If their food—spider mites—does become scarce, they will simply starve or move along.

Many people wonder why they experience a spider mite outbreak just after spraying pesticides on their trees. Research on mites has shown that when they're exposed to certain pesticides (carbaryl and parathion), they will reproduce much faster than they normally would.

If you live in a dry area, it's important to sprinkle water on pathways around trees and gardens, in order to keep dust down. Spider mites, like other species of mites, love dry, dusty conditions, so adequate watering is essential to keep them away.

A simple spray of water from a hose can dislodge the mites from their host plants and reduce their population. Be sure to really blast the underside of the leaves, too. If plain water isn't reducing the mite population enough, some of the new insecticide soaps on the market are good at controlling mites. Read the label and follow all instructions carefully, because some soaps can burn plants. If overhead watering (as opposed to ground or drip watering) is feasible in your garden, it will help keep mite populations down. This method is used successfully to control mites on grapes in the West.

When spider mites are a problem on house plants, one method that is effective is to rub a cotton swab dipped in equal parts water and alcohol on the plant. If the infestation is mild, this is usually all that is necessary to control the beasts. Rinse the plant well after treatment to prevent burning.

Mite life

Mites are very small (about $\frac{1}{50}$ inch) and sometimes completely invisible on first inspection. Most people notice the damage done by mites before they notice the mites themselves. Generally, when mite damage reaches a noticeable level, you are talking about an infestation of millions of mites.

Mites belong to the same arthropod order as ticks (*Acari*) and are not insects. Spider mites are related to other pest mites such as red mites, harvest mites (also known as chiggers or red bugs), and water mites. All mites have eight legs instead of the insect's six legs.

Spider mites are usually a pale yellow or green in color. Much like bees, spider mites are able to determine the sex of their offspring. An unfertilized egg will become a male and a fertilized egg will become a female.

Mite populations fluctuate as weather conditions change. When the weather is warm and dry, the mites will multiply rapidly, sometimes going through ten or more generations in one summer. Cool and damp conditions greatly reduce the numbers of mites.

TOMATO HORNWORMS

You can't wait for the first tomato of the season, and every day you check your prized tomato vines, waiting for that hard-earned fruit. On a visit to your garden one day, you're horrorstruck to discover that a section of leaves is missing. What could do that? A closer look reveals black pellets on some of the leaves and on the ground. Surprise—you have a tomato hornworm lurking.

Taking the worm by the horns

Tomato hornworms are equipped with excellent camouflage, making them very hard to see at first glance. Stay in the area of the droppings, and soon you'll see a motionless caterpillar hanging onto a stem. These large caterpillars can be controlled quite well by hand-picking.

A larger infestation may require additional treatment. A commercially available bacterium (*Bacillus thuringiensis*) is very effective against hornworms and other caterpillar species, such as cabbage loopers. When sprayed on plants, the bacterium invades the caterpillars and kills them. It works best on small caterpillars, so some of the large hornworms may not be killed quickly and will still need to be picked off by hand.

The hornworm spends the winter in a pupal form in the ground. Turning over the soil after you pull up the plants helps to bring these large brown pupae to the surface, where they can be discarded or left to be eaten by birds.

Hornworms have some natural predators, such as the *Trichogramma* and *Bracondiae* wasps. To check if you have any of these natural predators working in your yard, examine the backs of hornworms for attached white cocoons that look like fuzzy rice. Soon the cocoons will break open to reveal a small wasp that will search for another hornworm to lay its eggs on. When these eggs hatch, the larval wasps will feed on the hornworm caterpillar.

The life of a sphinx

The dreaded hornworm is really the immature form of the beautiful sphinx moth (*Manduca quinquemaculata*). This usually nocturnal moth is quite large, with one species having a wingspan of 5 inches or more. They have long, narrow front wings, with a heavy body that tapers at both ends. The sphinx moth has been compared with the hummingbird and is even called the "hummingbird moth" in some areas, because its feeding method resembles the bird's. The sphinx moth has a long proboscis, or tube, extending from its mouth, which it uses to suck nectar out of flowers.

The sphinx moth lays its pale green eggs on tomato plants as well as potato and tobacco plants. Soon the eggs hatch into hornworms, the larval form. So far we don't know if the horn-like structure from which the hornworm got its name serves any real purpose, except perhaps to scare off potential predators. Hornworms, which also have a camouflaging striped pattern, can grow to 4 inches in length, so it doesn't take many to completely wipe out a tomato plant!

WHITEFLIES

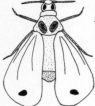

Clouds of tiny white insects are appearing around your garden plants. Your citrus trees have a blackened appearance due to a sooty mold on the leaves, and your hibiscus has white sheets of thick webbing hanging down under its leaves. It sounds like this little fly has taken over your yard.

Battling a tiny enemy

Many of the same methods for controlling aphids, such as the yellow sticky traps described on page 22, will also work for whiteflies. Stake the traps at plant level, out of direct sun, for best results. Replace when dirty.

Nasturtiums are a favorite of whiteflies, and planting some may keep the whiteflies happy and away from your other prized plants. Marigolds, planted in and around the garden, are also known to be a good whitefly repellent.

Natural predators like lacewings and ladybird beetles feed heavily on whiteflies. *Encarsia formosa*, a commercially available parasite, feeds on the whitefly in its nonmobile nymph stages. Hand-picking the most heavily infested leaves off the plant will give the beneficial predators a greater chance of controlling the pests.

Giant whiteflies are a big problem in California, but a new predatory wasp discovered in Mexico this year may provide some effective biological control in the near future.

Many gardeners rely on a strong spraying of water to greatly reduce the whitefly population. If stronger measures are needed, a soapy water spray or even a commercial insecticidal soap spray may be in order. Treating the underside of leaves is very important. Always check for burning with any soap product, and rinse the plant if necessary.

A water-alcohol solution is known to be an effective control for whiteflies. This spray also works well on house plants that can't stand the strong hose spray method. You can also dab the solution on house plants with a cotton ball.

A small vacuum cleaner will suck up many nymphs and adults on your plants. Vacuuming works best in the morning, when the whiteflies are cold and moving slowly. First, vacuum up some boric acid (a couple of tablespoons will do) to kill the flies when

> **• Whitefly control spray •**
>
> 1 cup water
> ³/₄ cup alcohol
> Mix and spray on plants.
> Check for burning before treating the entire plant. Rinsing the plants after the spray has been on for a few minutes will help reduce the chance of burning.

they arrive in the vacuum bag, or place the vacuum bag containing the whiteflies in a plastic bag in the freezer to kill them.

A commercial oil emulsion spray is one method for controlling whiteflies in large citrus trees. These are oils made from petroleum that kill whiteflies on contact by suffocation. However, oils are not species-specific and will harm the beneficial insects with which they come into contact. As with all methods of control for whiteflies, treating the undersides of leaves is very important. There are several oils on the market for this purpose. Many gardeners like to use a paraffinic oil, but check with your local nursery for the one that fits your gardening needs. Experts recommend avoiding the use of oils in very hot weather—you could literally fry the leaves on your plant.

Little fly, big trouble

These tiny ($1/12$ inch) flies are closely related to aphids and scale insects. Whiteflies are found worldwide and have been quite a problem for citrus growers in Florida and California. Cultivated crops, such as lettuce, have also been hit hard by whiteflies in recent years. Whiteflies are so named because of the fine white powder that covers their wings and bodies.

Whiteflies start their lives as tiny eggs ($1/100$ inch long) attached by short stalks to the underside of host plants. The nymphs hatch in four to twelve days and are called "crawlers." In this stage the whitefly is able to move about on the plant. The crawlers soon begin feeding on the plant by inserting their piercing mouth parts. After feeding and growing, the nymphs molt to a legless form, which is a flattened oval resembling a scale or mealybug. The whitefly goes through two more molts and then emerges as an adult. Three to four generations are produced in a season. The whitefly's unusual life cycle makes it one of the most difficult pests to treat.

PET HELP

FLEAS

Welcome to flea season! It seems the little bloodsuckers have taken over both house and yard. Your pets are scratching and biting themselves, and you and your children also suffer flea bites while playing with the family dog.

Help is on the way

Fleas have always been a major problem for humans and animals; it's estimated that Americans will spend $350 million on flea-fighting chemicals this year alone. In the past, DDT was routinely prescribed to fight fleas, and people throughout the ages have gone to great lengths to rid themselves of this dangerous pest. (One old recommendation was to mop wood floors with kerosene.) Following are some less drastic, helpful ideas to keep those pesky fleas under control:

In areas of the house where pets are allowed, a sprinkling of borax on the carpets and under the pet's bed will help keep flea numbers down by desiccating (drying out) the fleas. Sprinkle the borax on by hand, or place it in a flour sifter for a nice even application. Brushing the borax into the carpet gets the drying agent deep into carpet fibers where the flea eggs and larvae like to live. Leave it down for several hours (or even several days for heavy infestations)

> When using any product (like diatomaceous earth or borax) that contains dust particles, *always* wear a protective dust mask to avoid inhaling any potentially harmful particles, and *never* dust when children and pets are present.

and then vacuum it up. It is best to keep children and pets off the carpet while the borax is down. Use the borax treatment every time you vacuum during peak flea season for best results.

Diatomaceous earth, like borax, can also kill fleas by drying them. It has an added bonus in that it can also puncture an insect's outer waxy exoskeleton and cause even more moisture loss. Diatomaceous earth is made up of diatoms (silica "shells" of tiny one-celled organisms) that have settled on the ocean floor and fossilized into dried mineral layers, which are very powdery. **Note:** Do not use the form of diatomaceous earth intended for swimming pool filters. It is very coarse and chemically treated and is potentially harmful to the lungs of humans and pets. For use in the home or garden, choose only natural diatomaceous earth or food grade diatomaceous earth.

When vacuuming, remember to change your vacuum bag often, or even every time you vacuum if you have a heavy infestation. The vacuumed dust is perfect nourishment for the flea larvae you've just vacuumed into the bag. If you don't change the bag, you could be spreading fleas the next time you vacuum. To avoid changing the bag every time you vacuum, vacuum up a couple of tablespoons of boric acid or borax, which will kill the flea larvae and adults that enter the bag.

• Lemon flea repellent •

The peel of 2 large or 4 small lemons

1 quart water

Boil the lemon peels in the water for ten minutes. Cool. Sponge the lemon water on your pet and leave on for an hour or so. Rinse off. For heavy infestations, leave the lemon water on without rinsing. Repeat weekly, if necessary.

D'limonene, a compound found in lemon peels, is a very effective repellent and insecticide for fleas (and for other types of insects as well). Veterinarians often recommend products containing this compound because, when properly diluted, treatment can even be safe for kittens and puppies. This easy homemade lemon solution relies on the natural repellent action of D'limonene. Note: Just like people, animals (especially cats) can have allergies to lemons or any food item. If your pet starts shaking or vomiting after application of the lemon solution, wash the solution off with a good shampoo. If the symptoms persist, get worse after washing, or are severe, consult your veterinarian immediately.

Eucalyptus can also be an effective flea repellent. Eucalyptus leaves or mulch placed under your pet's bed or house work just like cedar shavings to repel fleas. In areas that have eucalyptus trees, substituting eucalyptus shavings for cedar shavings could be quite a savings. Eucalyptus can also be made into a "tea" to be sprayed on your pet or around your pet's bedding or house to repel the fleas.

Our eucalyptus flea repellent recipe gives directions for making your own extract. You can also purchase eucalyptus oil or extract concentrate (at health food or pet stores) and mix it with water.

Flea combing can be an effective method of control, but the effort it takes to do it routinely sometimes makes the job seem impossible, especially if you have a long-haired pet. If you do decide to flea comb your pet, keep a jar of seventy percent alcohol or vinegar nearby and plunge your comb into it to kill the dislodged fleas. For effective combing, comb first with the grain and again against the grain of your pet's coat.

Beneficial nematodes, which can usually be purchased at pet and home supply stores in the spring, can be sprayed in your yard, where they'll attack immature fleas. Read the Nematodes section in Chapter 6 for more information.

A new product on the market is Program, the flea birth control pill. You give the pill to your pet once a month, and when an adult flea bites your pet for a meal, it also gets a dose of an insect development inhibitor. This inhibitor prevents any eggs laid by

---

• Eucalyptus flea and tick repellent •

About 20 fresh eucalyptus leaves

1 quart of water

Boil leaves in the water for 5 to 10 minutes. The liquid should have a strong eucalyptus odor. Cool, strain out leaves, and spray on the liquid as necessary (pay special attention to your pet's feet). Some trees have stronger scents than others, so you may need to experiment with the number of leaves you use.

---

the adult from maturing and hatching. Studies done in Australia using Program showed a ninety-five percent reduction in the flea population at the end of the study. Program is only available through a veterinarian and since it only prevents future off-spring, you still must treat the remaining adults on your pet.

Another new product is methoprene, a flea-specific hormone you spray outdoors. When immature fleas are exposed to this hormone, they die without reproducing.

A flea's hungry life

Have you ever gone on vacation, or closed a resort house for the winter, only to find fleas waiting for you when you returned? Adult fleas that have had a host meal can live fifty to one hundred days without further food. Amazingly, adult fleas that have never eaten can live as long as two years without food.

Fleas are wingless, long-legged, jumping insects that live as parasites on animals. There are approximately 1,100 species of fleas worldwide, and they are easily identified by their bodies, which are flattened from side to side. Adult fleas rely on their great jumping power to escape their enemies. It has been calculated that a flea can jump 200 times the length of its body, or about twelve inches. That would be like a cat jumping 14,400 feet! Most adult fleas are brown or black, while the larvae and eggs are whitish.

Eggs of the flea are usually laid on the host and fall into the dust and crevices of the host's home or bed. The eggs usually hatch in two to fourteen days. One adult female flea may lay up to 5,000 eggs in her lifetime. The larva of the flea, which is a scavenger feeding on organic debris from your pet, resembles a maggot. After the larval stage, which can last from one to five weeks, a silken cocoon is formed, in which the larva transforms into the common adult flea.

Adult fleas emerge from their cocoons very hungry. Their only food is blood, and the little vampires begin immediately to look for a host meal. Adult fleas will feed once a day if the blood of a host is available. Whereas with mosquitoes only the females bite, both male and female fleas will bite a host for a blood meal.

Flies

 We're all familiar with the irritating antics of the common housefly. The sound of flies loudly buzzing against a window and the sight of them landing on your food can drive you crazy. Unfortunately, there are many types of flies and each one of them has its own special way of tormenting you and your pets—especially horses. If you own horses, you've probably witnessed the constant aggravation flies can cause to the horse (and to you!). Some flies, such as stable flies and horn flies, will bite man or beast, while others only attack fruits and vegetables. The house fly, which is simply looking for a free meal, serves mainly to annoy us.

Sending the annoying visitor packing

What would the fly swatter business be without flies? Who hasn't run for the swatter when the sound of a buzzing fly is just too much to bear any longer? Many owners of farm and stable animals have waged a never-ending war on these flying creatures. It is a matter of fact that horses, antelope, bison, and deer will attract flies no matter how clean their habitats are. Those of you with horses and cattle already know this firsthand.

Generally, the war on flies has been pretty frustrating, but good news may be here to help keep those flies at bay. It looks like a zookeeper in San Diego has built a better fly trap. (And you can imagine the fly problem a zoo might have, if it were left untreated!) The zookeeper tried many commercial fly traps, all with mixed results. Finally, a breakthrough came when the keeper noticed that the flies, especially the housefly and bottle fly species, were really attracted to old ground meat. A chunk of meat was placed into a commercial plastic bag fly trap, which contained a fly pheromone attractant, and a better fly trap was born.

You can make your own version of this fly control method to use outdoors. Buy a hanging plastic bag fly trap with a pheromone attractant at your local nursery or home center. Many brands are available and any will do. After preparing the trap according to the package directions, add a large quarter-sized piece of hamburger to the bag. Now hang the bag wherever you find flies. Sometimes it takes a few days for the hamburger to have just the right odor. Try placing different amounts of hamburger in your trap too, until it's perfect for your needs.

A short life

The common housefly (*Musca domestica*) has one of the shortest life cycles of any insect. Its whole life, from egg to adult, lasts only six to twenty days, depending on the temperature of its environment. This makes the housefly an ever-present pest to man, but an important source of food for many other insects and birds. Unfortunately, the housefly is known to be a carrier of many serious diseases, such as typhoid fever, cholera, anthrax, and dysentery.

> To catch a fly in your hand, or better yet swat it with a fly swatter, try aiming at it from behind. Flies always take off backwards, a little tip that will help you get your fly.

Houseflies possess only sucking mouth parts and hence cannot eat anything solid. In order for the housefly to eat something solid, it first must dissolve the solid food into a liquid form. To do this, the fly places its saliva (or sometimes its stomach contents) onto the solid food to partially digest it. Then the fly sucks up the dissolved liquid food. In this way, germs are passed and carried from one source to another.

TICKS

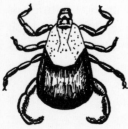

Let's say it's a beautiful day and you and your favorite four-legged friend have just returned from a nice walk. While taking off his leash, you notice a tick. There is no mistaking the small flattened-oval shape of these irksome arthropods.

Protecting yourself from ticks

Ticks are one of the hardest creatures to defend against because no matter how hard you try to repel them, you usually can't protect every area of your pet's (or your own) body. So carefully checking yourself and your pet after each outing is still a very wise idea.

During the summer months, when the weather is warm, we tend to wear less clothing. We don't like to go out wearing high boots with our pant legs tucked into them and long-sleeved shirts that are tight-fitting around the wrists and neck. But that's just the clothing necessary to guard against ticks. Loose-fitting clothing gives ticks good access to our bodies.

Ticks also love to get into places where your clothing will help them get a good hold on you. Some of their favorite spots are at the tops of socks, inside shirts, and under the loose elastic of your underwear. Knowing this, it is a good idea to check these areas frequently. Your pet, however, is not so lucky—any part of his body is fair game for a tick.

If you do find a tick on yourself or your pet, the best method of removal is to grab the tick with a tissue close to the skin and pull it straight out. Do not twist. Apply an antibiotic ointment to the site.

With the increased fear of Lyme disease, tick repellents are becoming very popular. Many on the market now have been shown to work quite well. DEET is a popular repellent used in small doses, but large doses of this compound can cause convulsions in pets and children, so care should be taken when using.

A popular natural repellent is citronella. (Yes, the same compound that works against mosquitoes.) Citronella is being used in some sunscreens, so these products will give you some mosquito and tick protection. Some products containing citronella also claim to protect against fleas.

Eucalyptus is an excellent repellent for ticks, fleas, and other insects, and you can make a simple and quite effective eucalyptus spray repellent (see page 53). Ticks are pretty resilient, so you may need to make the repellent a bit stronger. If making the repellent yourself is too much trouble, or if you live in an area that doesn't have eucalyptus trees, you can purchase eucalyptus oil in your local health food store and dilute it to the strength you want. Keep in mind when using this solution that some dogs, and especially cats, may not like the smell of eucalyptus. Start with a weak solution first and work up to a stronger-smelling solution if necessary.

Ticks are found throughout the United States, and precautions should be taken in your backyard to keep tick numbers down in heavily infested areas. Clearing away old, dead underbrush and keeping your lawn watered and closely mowed is helpful. Trapping and disposing of mice on your property will take away one of the tick's favorite hosts and hopefully send the tick packing elsewhere.

Can ticks make you sick?

Ticks are arthropods with eight legs; they're not true insects. (But who sits and counts the number of legs a tick has when he finds one on his pet?)

There are two families of ticks in the United States: hard ticks (*Ixodidae*) and soft ticks (*Argasidae*). They are all parasitic and attack mammals, birds, and reptiles. Besides the annoyance of being bitten by a tick, the bites can also be quite dangerous. Ticks transmit diseases, including Rocky Mountain spotted fever, Lyme disease, tularemia, and Texas cattle fever, to humans and animals.

Ticks are small creatures, about $3/16$ inch in length. They are usually dark brown to bluish gray in color. An engorged female may reach a length of ½ inch or more, and one female tick can lay 4,000 to 7,000 round brown eggs on the ground after she has fed on a host.

When the eggs hatch (about a month after they're laid), a tiny $1/40$-inch larva will climb up to the ends of blades of grass and other plants, to wait for some passing animal to climb onto. Once on board, the larva will feed on the animal (white-footed mice are a favorite of deer ticks at this stage) for about two to twelve days. The larva will then fall to the ground, shed its skin, and become a nymph. The nymph now looks for a host. After feeding for three to ten days on this host, again the nymph falls to the ground and undergoes its final change into the adult form. Now the adult is looking for you. It is only in the adult form that the tick attacks people. The entire life cycle of a tick can take two to three years.

In case you're unlucky enough to be bitten by a tick, you should know some of the symptoms of the serious illnesses they could carry in your area. Contact your doctor if you have any of these symptoms.

Lyme disease: rash, chills, fever, fatigue, arthritis-like stiffening in the joints, and severe headaches. Look for a bull's-eye red mark at the sight of the bite.

Rocky Mountain spotted fever: fever and a peculiar skin rash of grayish or brownish spots usually appearing on the arms, legs, and body a few days after the fever begins.

GOOD GUYS OR
BAD GUYS?

CENTIPEDES

You're out tending your garden one day, and as you move some debris, you see what looks like a multi-legged prehistoric creature running for cover. It has too many legs to be an insect, so what can it be? A better question is, is it beneficial or not? It's a good chance that creature is a centipede —and a great predator of insects and other small animals.

A good arthropod

The centipede is found worldwide in tropical and temperate climates. So far there are approximately 3,000 known species of centipedes (class *Chilopoda*) in the world. Most North American species range in size from 1 to 2 inches long and feed on small insects, slugs, and worms. However, centipedes in the tropical zones can reach lengths of 6 to 8 inches and feed on toads, snakes, and rodents.

Centipedes are characterized by one pair of legs coming out of each body segment, and most are brown in color. However, some are red, green, yellow, blue, or a combination of these colors. They are all somewhat flattened in shape and are usually nocturnal. Centipedes prefer to live in dark, damp places like under rocks, bark, and debris.

An old wives' tale says that the bite of the centipede can be fatal to humans. Even though centipedes do release a toxin from their powerful jaws to help them catch their prey, much like a venomous snake, no human death has ever been directly linked to a single bite from a centipede. The centipede's bite is said to feel like a very severe yellow jacket wasp sting.

It is unlikely that you can attract centipedes to your yard. But having some suitable habitat in your garden may help encourage any centipedes you already have to stay. An old board in a damp, shady spot might be all you need to keep a centipede on the prowl in your garden.

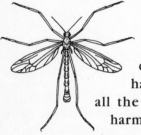

CRANE FLIES

Here they come—those giant flying "mosquitoes" that some people call mosquito hawks. Though they look like they could suck all the blood from a chihuahua, they're actually harmless.

Harmless imitators

The family of crane flies (*Tipulidae*) is a diverse group of over 1,450 species, ranging in size from tiny to more than three inches in length. They are long and slender, with narrow wings and long, fragile legs. Some species closely resemble mosquitoes, but crane flies do not bite. Adults possess a thin tube-like structure called a proboscis, which they use to feed on flower nectar, but very little is known about their feeding habits. Crane flies are not strong fliers and are often seen hovering in corners or bouncing against walls or windows.

Crane flies can be found in damp areas where there is plenty of vegetation. The larvae are mostly aquatic and feed on decaying plant matter. There is one species that does feed on living plants but the damage it causes is usually minimal. There are also a few beneficial species that prey on other insects.

Entomology students have gone to great lengths to try to preserve specimens of these delicate creatures, with little or no success. Many a student has opened his collection box only to find the poor creature's legs in pieces on the bottom of the box. With their delicate structure, it has long been a wonder that crane flies manage to exist at all.

CRICKETS

The cricket in your house may be happily chirping for a mate, but you're not happy to hear this sound in the middle of the night. You climb out of bed and head for the noise, but as soon as you are close enough to figure out where it is coming from, it stops, only to start again when you return to bed. After a few nights of this you're just about ready to call the sanitarium.

A sticky solution

To capture midnight chirping crickets in your house, you'll need duct tape and a few pieces of dry dog (or cat) food. Pull off a piece of tape about two to three feet long and place it sticky side up on the floor, along the baseboard where you hear the chirping. Now place pieces of dog food on the tape about eight inches apart. Crickets love dog food and when they walk on the tape to get the goodies, they should get stuck on the tape.

Many people believe crickets are good luck, so if you don't want to hurt the cricket, you can gently unstick him and deposit him outside where his chirping won't bother anyone.

Insect musicians

Male crickets and their cousins, the katydids, chirp to attract a mate and defend their territories. They do this by rubbing a structure called a file, located on their leg, with a structure on their wing, called a scraper. On warm nights the chirping of the males in search of a mate can go on for hours. Each cricket species sings a distinctive song, which a good listener can use to tell one cricket species from another.

The family to which crickets belong (*Gryllidae*) can be found throughout the United States. Crickets resemble small grasshoppers, but there is great diversity in the sizes and shapes they take. Ant-loving crickets are only 3 to 5 millimeters long and are found living in ant nests, whereas field crickets are close to an inch in length.

Crickets can cause damage to many field crops and in some areas have been recorded infesting fields in great numbers. Tree crickets can also cause serious damage to small tree limbs and twigs by girdling the twig with their egg laying. Most crickets overwinter as eggs, which are generally laid in the ground or in vegetation.

How hot is it?

Telling the temperature by using crickets as thermometers is a long-practiced art of naturalists and woodsmen. Try it out with the crickets in your neighborhood. Tree crickets or crickets caged off the ground give the best results because the ground is warmer than the air, and crickets on the ground will chirp the ground temperature they feel, instead of the air temperature you feel.

Two formulas for finding the Fahrenheit temperature are:

~ Count the number of chirps heard in fifteen seconds and add thirty-seven (some experts say to add forty) to the fifteen-second number. Try both numbers to see which one is right in your area.

~ Count the number of chirps heard in sixty seconds and subtract fifty. Divide that number by four, and then add fifty.

DARKLING BEETLES (AKA STINKBUGS)

What are those big black beetles that some people call stink bugs? Are they eating my garden? With their size, they must be doing a lot of damage.

Stinky scavengers

Darkling beetles may have committed the ultimate insult when they first raised their behinds toward menacing humans and emitted a black fluid with a very disagreeable odor. Since then they've been stuck with the awful name stinkbug.

Most of the 1500 species of darkling beetles that live in North America are either plant eaters, fungus eaters, or scavengers (on decomposing wood or dead animal matter). For the most part, the big black beetles we see are scavengers of dead matter. They are very common under stones, garbage cans, and loose bark. The beetle usually doesn't do any harm to gardens, but instead is seeking shelter and dead material in the garden. However, a few of the smaller species have been known to become plant pests. Tidy gardens usually have very few darkling beetles.

In arid regions, the darkling beetle has taken over for the carabid or ground beetle, which preys on many pests. In this case, the darkling beetle can be very beneficial.

The larva of the darkling beetle is greatly prized commercially—they're the mealworms we buy for fish bait and supplemental bird food.

Darkling beetles have no wings, and their only defense mechanism is the smelly fluid they excrete. But certain species of darkling beetle raise their abdomens for a different reason. In the desert, where water is scarce, a darkling beetle will point its raised abdomen at an oncoming fog. The fog droplets condense on the beetle's abdomen, and when enough of them merge to form a water drop, it will run down the abdomen, straight into the beetle's mouth!

EUCALYPTUS LONG-HORNED BEETLES

You've noticed lately that the beautiful eucalyptus trees you planted in your yard aren't looking so good. On closer inspection, you find that lots of sap is running down the trunks of the trees, and the branches and leaves are wilting and discolored. Is it a fungus? Perhaps, but it's more likely the damage can be attributed to the beautiful but destructive eucalyptus long-horned beetle.

Stopping the bothersome borer

It's the larval form of this large, lovely beetle (*Phoracantha semipunctata*) that causes all the damage to eucalyptus trees. The boring activity under the bark and inside the tree makes treatment and eradication of the borer quite difficult. Most of the time you don't even know you have the borer until damage to the tree is visible.

Prevention and early intervention, when possible, are the best tactics. Check trees regularly for signs of borer attack. Start by looking under loose bark for borer eggs, entrance holes, and tunneling. The tunneling will look like the wood has been burned with a branding iron; dark brown tunnels will radiate from a central area and suddenly disappear. Prune the limbs where these markings are found. Borers also love to attack stressed trees. A bit of extra water in the dry summer months and careful pruning of old and yellowing branches will help the tree remain strong and prevent an all-out borer infestation.

After pruning any areas of your eucalyptus trees where the borer has been found, be sure to seal all cuts to your tree and to dispose of the wood carefully. The borers can live in cut wood just as easily as live wood, so you may be raising the next generation of borer if you just leave the wood in a pile to dry. Many entomologists recommend that the wood should be buried or burned to prevent the spread of the borer. However, if you like eucalyptus wood for your fireplace and don't want to completely dispose of it, remove as much bark from the cut logs and branches as you can and lay them on a clear plastic tarp. After stacking the wood, completely cover and seal it in the plastic and leave it for at least six months. This should kill most of the borers inside the tarp and keep any that are looking for a home outside.

A long-horned life from down under

The eucalyptus long-horned beetle belongs to the beetle family *Cerambycidae*, which has over 1,200 species in this country, all of which feed on plants or trees. This Australian beetle, introduced to California in the early 1980s, has been a growing problem. It has the potential for expanding to many areas outside of California where eucalyptus trees grow.

Most long-horned beetles have elongated cylindrical bodies and back-sweeping antennae that are often two to three times longer than the body. They range in size from ¼ inch to over 3 inches in length, with the adult eucalyptus long-horned beetle measuring a little over an inch. Many adult long-horned beetles are brightly colored, and these usually feed on flowers. The eucalyptus long-horned beetle is dark brown with a cream-colored zigzag band across its back, and feeds exclusively on eucalyptus wood.

The adult beetles lay their eggs in bark crevices, and when the eggs hatch, the larvae will tunnel under the bark for a bit and then bore into the wood. The mature cream-colored larvae of the eucalyptus long-horned beetle grow to about 1¼ inches in length and ⅓ inch in width. By looking at the borer's tunnels, you can help identify which family of borer you have infesting your trees. This is important information in determining which treatment should be used for borers. Eucalyptus long-horned beetle larvae produce a round hole when boring.

Since the eucalyptus long-horned beetle is an imported beetle from Australia, it didn't have any natural enemies when it arrived in the U.S. However, work is being done to introduce predators of the beetle to this country and provide some much-needed natural control.

JERUSALEM CRICKETS

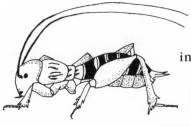

Sooner or later you'll see one, and it will take your breath away. The Jerusalem cricket is a large and ugly insect, but is it a friend or foe? It's so objectionable looking, it must be able to devour an entire garden, you think. But relax—it's a good guy to have around.

An ugly insect that really cleans up

The Jerusalem cricket belongs to the cricket subfamily *Stenopelmatinae*. This unusual cricket is found for the most part on the West Coast and is also known as a sand or stone cricket. It's wingless, nocturnal, and about 2 inches long, with a big head and stout legs. They don't look much like the common crickets we know at all, and they don't possess the ability to produce sounds, like their noisy cousins, the tree crickets. Jerusalem crickets do, however, possess a pair of powerful jaws that can inflict a nasty bite if a person handles one of them.

These large crickets are basically scavengers that will clean up old plants and debris around your yard by eating the dead and decaying plant material. Damage to gardens is minimal, if any, since they prefer brown plants to green ones. The crickets prefer loose soil and rocks they can hide under during the day. Being nocturnal, this cricket will remain unseen if the soil is left undisturbed.

The female Jerusalem cricket has mating habits similar to the female black widow spider's. After the female cricket mates with the male, she'll kill him, then lay her eggs in a case that she'll carry around until the young hatch.

SNAKES

It's hard to believe that those forked-tongued, legless creatures so many of us find a bit scary are beneficial. Even snakes that are venomous, like rattlesnakes, are predators who eat sizeable numbers of small animals. Snakes do the most good by helping to keep rodent populations down, thereby keeping rodents from invading our homes. Some snakes, like garter snakes, will even eat slugs and snails!

Uninvited guest

You generally won't know you have a snake visiting your yard until you actually see it yourself. For most people, this is not a pleasant experience. If you can't stand the thought of sharing your yard with a snake, then try one or all of the following ideas to make your yard less attractive to them.

Tack fine mesh wire to the bottom of your fence. For an extra measure of safety, bury the wire about six inches deep before tacking it to your fence. The wire should extend up the fence eighteen to twenty-four inches. This will also keep out other intruders, like bunnies and skunks.

Keeping a well-groomed yard can also deter snakes from taking up residency. Snakes like to hide under piles of mulch, brush, rocks, or wood to escape the summer sun. If you don't provide any shelter, they will soon be on their way. Be sure to plug up any holes or cracks leading under your house, too!

Eliminating the rodent population in your yard will keep snakes from thinking your yard is a delicatessen. Check out pages 12–14 for tips on rodent control.

Venomous snakes

Everyone is aware that the U.S. has its share of venomous snakes. The National Audubon Society's *Field Guide to North American Reptiles & Amphibians* lists 115 species of snakes in the United States, with only four kinds—rattlesnakes, coral snakes, water moccasins, and copperheads—classified as venomous. Good common sense (and an understanding of how they live, what they look like, and when they're active) will go a long way toward preventing a snake bite. But if you are bitten, some basic "snake first aid" knowledge will be very helpful.

~ Remain calm.

~ Try to immobilize the area, using a stick taped to an arm or leg, for instance.

~ Wash the bitten area with soap and water, if available.

~ Do not apply a tourniquet or ice to the bitten area.

~ Do not cut the bitten area. Sucking out the venom yourself isn't effective and may cause more problems. A Sawyer Extraction Pump is the only suction method recommended by most experts.

~ Send someone for help. If you are alone, walk (don't run) to the nearest phone and call for emergency help.

Slithering through life

Snakes are reptiles, which means they all have scales on their bodies, lay eggs, and are cold-blooded. Snakes also have no legs, ears, or eyelids. They can range from 6 inches to 8½ feet long and can be found in most habitats throughout the U.S.

Snakes survive and thrive because they are very effective predators. They possess specialized body parts specifically designed to help them catch their favorite prey: rodents. Most people don't know that a snake's tongue, which is usually in constant motion, is really a part of its nose. The snake picks up scent particles with its tongue and then slides it into a special organ, called the Jacobson's organ, on the roof of its mouth. This organ is connected to the olfactory nerve and the nose.

Another organ snakes rely on is the heat sensor or pit organ, which is located between the eyes and nose. Snakes that belong to the pit viper family of snakes (such as rattlesnakes) all have these organs. They use them to "see" an animal's body heat. This is how a pit snake can find and catch its prey in total darkness.

Snakes have no external ears, but they can feel vibrations through their jawbone and body. So they can actually feel someone coming, much like you can feel a train coming by touching the track.

Remember that snakes are among the good guys. If at all possible, encourage them to come to your yard, and you'll have fewer problems with pest species.

SPIDERS

Spiders are among the good guys; however, many people feel there is nothing more creepy than a spider hovering overhead in its web. There are more than 34,000 different spider species all over the world, and most of them are predaceous! Luckily, most of their victims are insects, which makes them a great asset for controlling the numbers of insects in our environment.

Good guys with a bad reputation

Spiders belong to the family of arachnids, and they differ from insects in various ways. All spiders have eight legs and two body segments, whereas all insects have six legs and three body segments. The spider's first body segment, called the cephalothorax, has the eyes, venom glands, legs, and fangs. The second segment, called the abdomen, contains the rest of the internal organs, plus the silk glands and spinnerets (from which the spider pulls its silk). Like insects, spiders molt: when the spider outgrows its skin, it will split the old skin off, to reveal a new one.

Spiders didn't always have a bad reputation. Hundreds of years ago, many people, believing spiders had the ability to ward off diseases, ate spiders or wore them around their necks. And today, scientists are looking at spider venom as a possible source of new medicines.

The average spider eats about 100 insects a year, and many eat more. In a one-acre field, you might find up to 10,000 spiders. That equals one million insects eaten in one year!

Though it's not uncommon to think of webs when one thinks of spiders, not all spiders spin a web. Some spiders use their "silk" for other purposes, instead of spinning a web to catch their dinner. A few build trap doors or funnels, one species uses its silk as a lasso to catch its prey, and some are hunters that actively run and catch their meals. No matter what method they use to catch their prey, spiders are excellent hunters!

All spiders possess a pair of fangs and venom to help them kill their prey. It is this venom that makes people respect and fear spiders. It should be mentioned, however, that if given a choice, a spider would not choose to bite a human but would save its venom for something it could actually eat!

Potentially dangerous spiders

The two North American spiders that are potentially dangerous to humans are the brown recluse and the black widow.

Fortunately, the black widow spider is easily recognized by the distinctive markings on its abdomen. A small red hourglass can be seen on the underside of its black abdomen. These spiders build messy webs that resemble cobwebs in wood piles, garages, and basements. The black widow spider has even been known to build a home in toys left outdoors. The venom of this spider is very powerful, but generally only a tiny amount is released. This usually only causes pain at the site and nausea in an adult; however, to a small child the venom can be quite dangerous, and a doctor should be called immediately.

The brown recluse spider is much harder to identify. It is a very shy spider that can be gray or brown and likes to live in warm, dry places. The recluse spider is also called the sweater drawer spider and the violin spider. The violin name comes from the small violin shape on its back. The name sweater drawer spider suggests one of its favorite hiding places, and one spot to watch out for it. Its bite isn't particularly painful and you may dismiss it as just another spider bite at first. However, soon the flesh next to the bite will start to rot. This process usually isn't painful but if left untreated, large holes can form in the skin and lead to serious problems.

It's good to know that the brown recluse spider will actually run and hide if it hears you coming. Most bites from the recluse spider occur when the spider is trapped or crushed next to the skin.

An old-fashioned remedy for ordinary spider bites

> **• Spider bite treatment •**
> Moisten tobacco from a cigarette, pipe, etc., and place it over the bitten area. Hold the tobacco against the skin for about 15 minutes or until the pain subsides.

What do you do when a spider bites you? If you fear you've been bitten by a black widow or brown recluse, you should seek professional medical assistance. However, if you've been bitten by an ordinary spider, try this old remedy to reduce the swelling and pain. It uses tobacco, long the method of choice for treating spider bites and scorpion stings.

SPITTLEBUGS
(FROGHOPPERS)

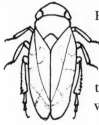Perhaps you've strolled through your garden or taken a leisurely afternoon hike through a meadow and seen what looks like spit in the branches of plants and grasses. No way are you going to look through the spit to see what it is! If you did, you'd see the very bizarre spittlebug or froghopper.

Danger in numbers

These small hopping insects are members of the *Cercopidae* family. They are greenish to brown in color and have an average length of ½ inch. The adults resemble tiny frogs, with stout heads and bulging eyes, hence the name froghopper. Their other name, spittlebug, comes from the immature nymph's habit of producing a spit-like substance that keeps it from drying out. The adult spittlebug has the ability to hop about freely on the plant and to fly in search of fresh succulent plants.

Several species of spittlebugs can cause serious damage to plants by stunting their growth. These insects, in large numbers, can use their piercing-sucking mouth parts to extract enough of the plant's juices to cause the plant to wilt and die. In the eastern part of the U.S., the meadow spittlebug (*Philaenus spumarius*) attacks clover, alfalfa, and strawberries, and causes a great deal of economic damage. There are also a couple of species of spittlebugs that damage pine trees. Spittlebugs do the greatest damage in areas that have high humidity.

Controlling the tiny spittlebug is a labor-intensive proposition. One of the best control measures is to cut them out of your plants when you see them. On hardier plants, a very strong stream of water may dislodge the creatures. On heavy crop infestations, one practice is to harvest the crop before the adults can lay their eggs in the late fall, then clean up any grasses or plants around the fields where the adults could lay eggs.

TARANTULA HAWK WASPS

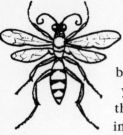

A very large black wasp with red/orange wings and long spiny legs just went whizzing by your head. What on earth could it be doing in your yard? Hopefully, it doesn't sting people, you think. Yes, it does sting, but most likely it is looking for a tarantula to feed to its young.

A tarantula's worst nightmare

Tarantula hawks are just one of the species in the spider wasp family (*Pompilidae*). This family of wasps is highly skilled at catching spiders to feed its developing larvae. Spiders eat both beneficial and pest insects, and the spider wasp's role is to keep the number of spiders in check. However, most gardeners would rather have spiders instead of insect pests, so it's up to you to decide whether you think spider wasps are beneficial or not.

You don't have to do anything special to attract tarantula hawks to your yard. If you have tarantulas roaming around, then you'll probably have tarantula hawks cruising your yard as well. If it spots a tarantula, the wasp will attack the big spider in its burrow. The wasp will sting the tarantula to paralyze it, and then deposit an egg on it. The spider remains alive but anesthetized. The wasp's egg will hatch and feed on the live spider until it is ready to spin a cocoon. An adult wasp will emerge from the cocoon to feed on flower pollen and search for more tarantulas.

YELLOW JACKET WASPS

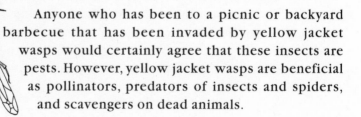

Anyone who has been to a picnic or backyard barbecue that has been invaded by yellow jacket wasps would certainly agree that these insects are pests. However, yellow jacket wasps are beneficial as pollinators, predators of insects and spiders, and scavengers on dead animals.

Help to avoid a stinging situation

Many of the wasp traps on the market today claim to keep those pesky dinner invaders at bay. Some are more effective than others, but most are based on the principle of attracting the wasps using a bait source, commonly a food attractant.

You can make your own bait using fruit juice (apple is a good choice) and a piece of meat. The trap itself can be made of many things: an old soda bottle, a plastic milk bottle, or even a plastic bag. The idea is to fill the trap container with fruit juice to a depth of about two inches. Then place a small piece of raw meat (like hamburger or fish) in the trap as well. Leave the lid off the bottle and place it out on your picnic table or, even better, on a table all by itself. Ants will also love this trap, but setting it in a pan of water will help deter them.

Now, as the fruit juice ferments and the meat spoils, the trap will give off an odor the wasp should love. The unsuspecting wasps will crawl into the bottle, fall into the juice, and drown. If you use plastic bags, cut a small hole near the top to allow the wasp to get in. Next, hang the bag, supporting the top in two places (an old wire coat hanger works well) for best results. A plastic bag trap similar to this can also be purchased in garden shops and camping centers if you don't want to make your own.

You can use the juice or the meat by itself in the trap, or try various combinations to get just the right bait—one that is irresistible to your neighborhood wasps. If you use meat alone, replace the juice with the same quantity of water, as you need liquid for the wasps to drown in.

Skunks have been known to raid ground wasp nests for wasp larvae. If you know of a ground wasp nest, pour some honey around the nest opening. The honey will attract the neighborhood skunks to the nest and the skunks can have a meal of honey and wasps.

Insect good guy, but a stinger to man

Yellow jacket wasps belong to the same wasp family (*Vespidae*) as hornets and paper wasps. This family of wasps is especially known for its powerful stinger, which the wasp can use over and over again (unlike the honeybee, which can only use its stinger once).

Paper wasps construct a large nest of many layers of paper, making individual hexagonal cells for the larvae. The wasps construct this nest by chewing wood or foliage, mixing it with saliva, and then applying the mixture as a sculptor would. Nests are usually found in protected areas like tall trees or house eaves; some are built underground. An average nest may contain from 5,000 to 25,000 wasps in the summer. Each nest will have a single queen. Unlike bees, most wasp colonies do not live through the winter. Instead only the female queen overwinters and builds a new nest in the spring.

Adult wasps generally feed on flower nectar and play an important part in pollination for many species of plants. The larvae are fed lots of insects and scavenged pieces of dead animal. It is when the wasps are scavenging for meat to feed their larvae that they become most annoying to humans.

BENEFICIAL INSECTS AND ANIMALS

BATS

Bats are one of the most maligned animals of all time. Who doesn't think of a bat when they hear the word vampire? Many people still think of bats as dirty bloodsuckers that fly through the night looking for victims. Of course, in the United States people are starting to know better. Here, bats are the heroes of the gardener: they are valuable pollinators, and they also consume large quantities of insects each night. Insect-eating bats usually catch their prey in midair, and disappear without a sound, so many people have bats in their yards and probably don't realize they do.

It's great to have a bat about the house

Bats are nocturnal and many are crepuscular, which means they are active at dawn and dusk. They spend their nights searching for food, mostly insects like beetles, moths, leafhoppers, and mosquitoes. A colony of 150 big brown bats can protect farmers in the area from up to eighteen million or more rootworms each summer. Just imagine how much work it would take for the farmers to protect their crops from rootworms if it weren't for the bats! Unfortunately, bats are indiscriminate feeders that will eat whatever insects they find. We like to think they only eat pest insects but they will take their share of beneficial insects as well.

One area in which bats excel is mosquito and gnat control. A single little brown bat can catch 600 mosquitoes in one hour. If you have ever been in a cloud of gnats, imagine that cloud ten times worse without bats. In areas with high numbers of mosquitoes, people have been putting up bat houses to encourage bats to roost nearby.

A bat house is easy to make and resembles a bird house with an entrance in the bottom. There are many plans available for bat houses but the one shown on the following two pages, from Bat Conservation International in Austin, Texas, incorporates simple construction, light weight, and low cost.

When you've finished building the house, hang the box at least fifteen to twenty feet off the ground. Before you know it, you'll have a bat (or bats) roosting. If building the house is too much trouble, you can order a ready-made house from Bat Conservation International by calling their catalog number, (800) 538-BATS.

In addition to eating insects, bats are excellent pollinators, a fact that has been overlooked by many. In rainforest ecosystems, bats play a key role in flower pollination and seed dispersal for many trees and shrubs. Many of the tropical fruit trees grown in the U.S. also depend on bat pollination. Avocados, agave plants (from which tequila is produced), bananas, mangoes, cashews, dates, and figs are just a few plants that benefit from bat pollination.

Bat guano (feces) is also an excellent fertilizer. One study suggests that bat guano will actually reduce pesticide residue in the soil. The bacteria in the guano is now being used to detoxify wastes, improve detergents, and produce gasohol and antibiotics.

Sometimes a bat will take up residency in an attic or the eaves of a house. In these cases, the bat becomes an unwanted guest, and screening off that particular area is the best way to send him on his way. Wait for the bat to leave to feed before placing the screening.

Hanging around with bats

Bats are members of the *Chiroptera* group of mammals. They are the only true flying mammals, and some estimate they have been flying for about sixty million years. They accomplish this feat by flying with their "hands." The hand of the bat forms the wing. A thin membrane stretches between the finger bones and extends down the hand bones to the forearm, and another membrane attaches the hind legs and tail.

There is some disagreement about bats' eyesight. Most people think bats are blind (hence the old saying, "blind as a bat"). Bats do indeed have small eyes, but they aren't blind. However, scientists do agree that bats' vision is probably not needed when they use echolocation (a type of sonar) to locate their food. When bats fly,

> The twenty million Mexican free-tailed bats that live in Bracken Cave in Texas eat 250 tons of insects in a single summer night!

they emit high-frequency sounds that bounce back from objects around them. Their sensitive ears pick up the sounds, and they can translate these sounds and find their food.

Bats can be found thoughout the continental United States. About forty percent of American bat species are in severe decline, with many listed as threatened or endangered. The little brown bat has a range of just about the entire United States. It is also the world's longest-lived mammal for its size; it has a life span which often exceeds thirty-two years. Most bats are brown to black in color, and all hang with their heads down when at rest.

Some bats migrate, while others do not. One species has been known to travel over 1,000 miles between their summer and winter homes. Those bats that do not migrate hibernate in their roosts. There, they go into torpor for the winter (unlike hummingbirds, which go into torpor each and every night!).

Most bat litters consist of one or two young per year, which are born in May or June. This slow reproduction rate makes the bat exceptionally vulnerable to extinction. The young, called pups, stay with their mothers for about a month, by which time they are able to fly and feed themselves.

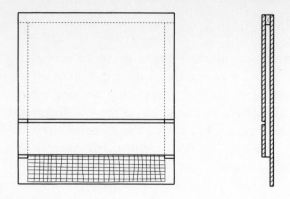

Small Economy Bat House

Materials Needed (makes 1):
- $1/4$ sheet (2' x 4') $1/2$" cdx (outdoor grade) plywood
- 1 piece 1" x 2" (0.75" x 1.75" finished) x 8' pine (furring strip)
- $1/8$" mesh hdpe (plastic) netting, 20" x 22.5" [such as Internet product #XV-1670 (1-800-328-8456)]
- 20-30 $1 5/8$" multipurpose (drywall) screws
- 1 pint latex acrylic paint
- 1 tube paintable acrylic caulk
- $5/16$" staples

Recommended tools:
- table saw
- scissors
- stapler
- paintbrush
- caulking gun
- variable speed reversing drill
- Phillips bit for drill
- tape measure or yardstick

Construction procedure:

1. Measure and cut plywood into three pieces:
   26.5" x 24" • 16.5" x 24" • 5" x 24"

2. Measure and cut furring into one 24" and two $20 1/4$" pieces.

3. Screw back to furring, caulking first. Start with 24" piece at top.

4. Staple the netting to inside surface of back, starting at the bottom. Be sure netting lies flat (curve down) and does not pucker.

5. Screw front to furring, top piece first (don't forget to caulk). Leave $1/2$" vent space between top and bottom front pieces.

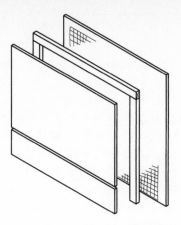

6. Caulk around outside joints if needed to seal roosting chamber.

7. Attach a 3" x 28" board to the top as a roof if desired.

8. Paint exterior at least twice.

Modifications to the Small Economy Bat House:

1. Wider bat houses can be built for larger colonies. Be sure to adjust dimensions for back and front pieces, ceiling furring strip, and netting. A $3/4$" support spacer may be required in the center of the roosting chamber for bat houses over 24" wide.

2. Two bat houses can be placed back-to-back mounted on poles. A horizontal $3/4$" slot should be cut in the back of each house about 10" from the bottom edge of the back piece to improve ventilation and permit movement of bats between houses. Make this cut before assembly. Two 4" pieces of wood screwed horizontally to each side will join the two boxes. Cover with two 3" x 22" vertical boards. One 3" x 22" vertical piece attached to each side over the horizontal pieces blocks light but allows bats and air to enter. Leave a $3/4$" space between the two houses, and roughen the wood surfaces or cover the back of each with plastic netting. Do not cover the vents. A tin roof covering both houses protects them and helps prevent overheating. Eaves should be about 3" in southern areas and about $1^1/2$" in the North.

3. Ventilation may not be necessary in colder climates. In this case, the front should be a single piece 23" long. Smaller bat houses should not be used in northern areas.

Hands off

Though all mammals can contract rabies, the reporting of rabid bats often makes the evening news. The estimate of bats that actually do contract rabies is less than one-half of one percent of all bats. Even though this number is very small, it should still serve as a warning to never pick up a bat off the ground. Grounded bats are usually sick or injured and will not appreciate being picked up. If you do find a grounded bat that must be moved or disposed of, use a shovel to pick it up. Place the bat in a bucket or a hard-sided box with a lid. (Bats can bite through a plastic bag.) Many areas require you to report grounded bats, so contact the agriculture officials in your area for advice.

BEES

 Everyone knows how beneficial bees are in pollinating fruit, vegetables, and flowers. Although many of us have great respect for the job the honeybee does, most of us are still afraid of the bee's sting. With all the recent reports of the potential threat of the Africanized honeybee ("killer bee"), the fear of bees is rising.

The truth about Africanized bees:

~ Killer bees are not giants—they're slightly smaller than the ordinary European honeybees we commonly see.

~ An individual Africanized honeybee flying or pollinating a flower will not pose a threat to people.

~ Killer bees are most defensive when disturbed or provoked near their hive.

~ Killer bees are ten times more likely to sting than European honeybees, but like the European bees they can only sting once.

~ Africanized honeybee venom is no more toxic than European honeybee venom.

- Eliminating nesting sites on your property can reduce bee problems.

- You can possibly outrun a killer bee attack if you run at full speed (15 mph) for ⅛ to ¼ of a mile.

- It has been estimated that it would take about 1100 bee stings to kill an average adult.

- Wear light-colored clothing and avoid perfumes around possible Africanized nests to reduce your chance of an attack.

- If you are attacked, cover your head and move inside a building or car immediately.

Keeping bees in their place

Africanized honeybees have expanded their territory an average of 200 miles per year since their unfortunate escape from a Brazilian test site in 1957. The bees do this by swarming. When a hive is getting crowded, it sends a signal to the workers to produce a new queen. The new queen, along with a large number of the workers, will leave the old hive to establish a new one. During the swarm, scout bees are on the lookout for a suitable new hive site. European bees also swarm, but Africanized bees swarm more frequently because their hives are smaller and reach capacity more quickly.

Another difference between European and Africanized honeybees is that Africanized bees will establish a hive in the ground, whereas European bees prefer a raised hive. This habit of ground hives requires the public to be on the alert. The simple act of mowing the lawn near a hive could send an Africanized colony into a frenzy. Parents and adults need to check their property carefully for potential ground hive sites and destroy them. Any opening bigger than one inch is a potential hive; for example, old burrows (from rabbits or other animals) can be taken over by the bees. In Arizona, meter readers have to be extremely careful when removing meter plates, because several Africanized hives have been found in meter boxes.

Africanized bees are excellent honey producers, even in times of poor flower production, and it was once thought that cross-breeding the less aggressive European bees with the Africanized bee would produce a bee that would be a superior honey producer.

A honey of a deal

Humans have been robbing bees of their sweet irresistible honey for all of recorded history. Rock paintings of honey gathering found in Spain date back to 7,000 B.C. The art of modern beekeeping has come a long way since then: today, honeybees can be found and kept in most areas of the world, except the polar regions.

> Bees make 60,000 nectar-collecting trips to flowers to produce just one teaspoon of honey!

Most people do not realize that prior to 1500 the common honeybee (*Apis mellifera*) only lived in the Old World: Europe, Africa, and Asia. As new lands were colonized, settlers brought along many of their favorite animals, like horses and bees. The first record of bees being established in North America was in 1638. Our native North American bees do not produce the elaborate hives of the European bees, nor do they have the honey-producing potential.

Bees were first brought to the new world to produce honey and wax. It wasn't until this century that the bee's importance as a pollinator was appreciated. In California alone, forty-two different nut, fruit, vegetable, forage, and seed crops, with an estimated annual revenue of $1.5 billion, rely directly on bee pollination. Even the world's most important forage crop for animals, alfalfa, depends on cross-pollination by bees.

In the past, bees were often used to forecast the weather. When bees stored a lot of honey in the fall, people believed it indicated a severe winter to come. It can be said that bees are and have long been a part of our everyday lives.

HOVER FLIES (SYRPHID FLIES)

You see little flying insect "helicopters" all over your flowers—they seem to hover motionless, resembling small hairless bees. What could they be, and what are they doing in your yard?

Flower flies

This interesting fly is one of the gardener's greatest allies. The hover fly (called the "flower fly" by many) belongs to the fly family *Syrphidae*, one of the largest families, with 940 species in North America. Many of these flies are brightly colored and resemble various types of bees, wasps, and bumblebees. Though they look like insects that are capable of stinging, hover flies are harmless to people. Because they mimic stinging insects, many other predators (including birds) will leave them alone.

To know for sure if you have hover flies or bees, check the number of wings. Hover flies are true flies and only have two wings, while bees have four wings. Many hover flies also have abdomens that are flattened from top to bottom, unlike true bees, which have very round abdomens.

The adult hover fly feeds on flower nectar, which makes it an excellent pollinator and a great asset to every garden. An added bonus is that the larvae of some hover fly species are great predators as well. One of their favorite types of prey is aphids, although they also like mealybugs and other small insects. The worm-like larvae possess large fangs which they use to grab their prey and drain the fluids from their bodies, in much the same way that lacewing larvae do.

Female hover flies will lay their eggs right in the midst of an aphid colony. In aphid control, only the ladybird beetle larva (or aphid lion) is more effective than the hover fly larva. In some hover fly species, the larvae are scavengers that live in the nests of ants, bees, and wasps.

GREEN LACEWINGS

Gardeners have long enjoyed having green lacewings in their gardens. Many have marvelled at their beauty and grace, not knowing it's the larvae of this insect that are great to have around.

A lion of a predator

Those delicate-looking insects are definitely wolves in sheep's clothing. The larval form is a fierce-looking, voracious aphid predator, aptly nicknamed the aphid lion. Though it also eats mites, mealybugs, and other small insects, its primary target is aphids.

The aphid lion almost appears to be a cross between an earwig (both have large mandibles) and a ladybird beetle larva (both have large spiny abdomens). The lacewing larva first uses its large mandibles like tongs to grab its prey; next, the mandibles do double duty and suck the juices from the victim.

If you think this paints an ugly picture of these larvae, you'd be right. Many a new gardener has killed this larval insect because it looks like it must be harmful. Some gardeners say they look like alligators, with sickle-like mouth parts. Lacewing larvae have even been known to place the dried bodies of their victims on top of their own bodies as camouflage, to be better able to sneak up on their prey.

Lacewing eggs can be purchased by mail order, or sometimes large nurseries will order them for you. A small list of suppliers can be found in the mail order section at the end of this book.

A delicate life?

The lacewing belongs to the order of insects called *Neuroptera* (meaning nerve wing). Adult lacewings possess four beautifully clear, delicate wings, which are all equal in size. Lacewings have veins resembling fine lace criss-crossing through their wings, hence their name. When at rest, this insect holds its wings roof-like over its body.

The adults range in size from ½ to ¾ inch and have striking golden eyes. There are also brown lacewings, and their larval form is also predaceous. Adult lacewings are not predators, but instead feed on honeydew, as well as pollen and nectar from plants.

Lacewings can be found in many types of foliage, including grasses, trees, and shrubs. They will search out aphid colonies and lay their eggs among them. Lacewing females lay their eggs on long, thin stalks on the underside of leaves, because otherwise the first larvae to hatch would cannibalize the other eggs upon hatching. Instead, the newly hatched larva eats the stalk, giving the rest of the eggs a chance to hatch.

Be aware that, as beautiful as lacewings are, they can give off a very unpleasant odor if handled or disturbed.

If you live in the western states or are planning a trip there soon, keep your eyes open for snakeflies, a special member of this order. These ½-inch-long insects look like black lacewings but with one difference: like praying mantids, snakeflies can move their heads. Very few insects have this ability. If you happen to see snakeflies on a warm evening, when they're drawn toward a light, you might swear they're looking right at you. Snakefly larvae also prey on small insects, such as aphids.

GROUND BEETLES (CARABID BEETLES)

 Ground beetles, which range in length from ¼ to 1 inch, are great nocturnal predators that like to hide under logs, stones, bark, and soil in the daytime. They are usually black and shiny, but some can be marked by bright colors. Most gardeners don't know how good these little beetles are for pest control.

How good are they?

Both the adults and the larvae are excellent predators. Another name for this beneficial beetle is the predaceous ground beetle. Some of their favorite insect meals are cutworms, grubs, root

maggots, and other soft-bodied pests found both ab[ove and] below the soil. Some species of ground beetles love to [eat] slugs and snails as well. When these beetles are disturb[ed they] will run quickly and seldom fly.

To ensure a good supply of ground beetles in you[r garden,] provide a place for them to hide. Place a board or log at [the edge] of your garden. Check under the hiding place often to s[ee you] do indeed have ground beetles working for you. Provid[ing a hid-]ing place sometimes encourages other pest species [(such as] snails and slugs) to congregate there, but the beetles [are] happy to have a meal deliver itself.

Knowing the good guy

Ground beetles belong to *Carabidae*, the second large[st family] of beetles in North America, with 2,500 species. With [the huge] numbers of beetles in the world—about a quarter of [all insect] species known so far and about 29,000 species just [in North] America—how do you tell if you have a predaceous gr[ound bee-]tle and not a potential pest in your garden?

To identify what type of beetle you have, first catc[h it in a] jar. By looking closely at the antennae and wing cove[rs with a] small magnifying lens, you can distinguish predaceou[s ground] beetles from other beetles. The antenna segments of th[e ground] beetle will all be the same length, and the antennae th[emselves] will be attached on the sides of the beetle's head bet[ween the] eye and the mandible or jaw. Most ground beetles will [have] longitudinal grooves or rows of punctures on their wi[ng covers] (called elytra).

One famous type of ground beetle is the bombardi[er beetle,] which ejects what looks like a puff of smoke from its [rear. This] smoke pops and vaporizes into a cloud when it comes [in con-]tact with air. This trick makes a great distraction defen[se, much] like the octopus' ink cloud.

Another well-known ground beetle, the caterpilla[r hunter,] was imported from Europe to fight the gypsy moth, a [serious] tree pest. But beware—this brightly colored green and [gold bee-]tle gives off an offensive odor when handled.

Y'all come back

To ensure that hover flies keep coming back to your garden, plant plenty of nectar-rich flowers, which the adults love. Border plantings of daisies, sunflowers, marigolds, and an assortment of your area's native flowers will ensure hover flies keep visiting your garden for the entire season.

HUMMINGBIRDS

Long before the common honeybee was imported into this country from Europe, hummingbirds were hard at work pollinating flowers here. These small dynamos must visit approximately 1,022 fuschia flowers to supply the 6,600 to 12,400 calories they need each day to survive. Each hummingbird will consume more than half its total weight in food each day, and a big part of that will be insects. The insects provide protein, minerals, vitamins, and fats, which are essential nutrients for the birds.

> If a 170-pound man were a hummingbird, he would need to consume about 155,000 calories each day (310 Big Macs, for example) in order to stay alive.

Life as a hummingbird

Hummingbirds, those small jewels at your feeder, are some of the world's most intriguing birds. They hold many records of the bird world, including:

~ The smallest bird in the world. The bee hummingbird weighs only 2.5 grams!

~ They are the only birds whose wings beat in a figure-eight pattern, allowing them to hover and fly backwards rapidly. The smaller species (there are a total of 342 hummingbird species worldwide) have an average wing beat of eighty beats per second and up to 200 beats per second during courtship displays.

~ At night, hummingbirds regularly go into a form of hibernation called torpor. Chilean hummers were once called "resurrection birds" because they appeared to rise from the dead each morning.

~ They have the highest normal body temperature of any bird, up to a whopping 106 degrees Fahrenheit.

~ Their hearts are the biggest in relation to their body size of all warm-blooded animals. Their heart rate can reach 1,260 beats per minute.

Inviting hummingbirds to your garden

Those of you who have hummingbirds darting about your garden already know the joys of watching them feed at a flower, or seeing them act like "big" bullies to other hummers who would like to share their territory. Making your yard an attractive place for hummingbirds to visit is simple and rewarding.

Plant flowering shrubs and vines that hummingbirds love. In the western U.S. there are about 130 species of plants that exhibit some adaptation for hummingbirds. Cape honeysuckle is a good example.

> • **Sugar solution for hummingbirds** •
> 1 cup warm water
> ¹/₄ cup white sugar
> Stir until sugar is dissolved, and immediately use in your feeder.

Hang a hummingbird feeder. San Diego Zoo hummingbird keepers recommend skipping the commercial sugar solutions and filling your feeder with this simple, inexpensive recipe.

Zookeepers caution you to avoid putting red food coloring in the water. It is unknown how the coloring affects the birds, so it's better to leave it out. Instead, buy a feeder with a red tip or one with a design of red flowers on the bottle (you can also paint the flowers on yourself). Put in only the amount of sugar water that the hummers will consume in two to four days to prevent mold from growing in your feeder and keep the sugar solution from turning rancid. If mold does grow, use toothpaste on a bottlebrush to clean inside the bottle or in hard-to-reach areas. A tablespoon of rice shaken inside will also help remove mold.

Ants are attacking your feeder

Now that you have hummingbirds coming to your yard, you will probably find that ants are flocking to the sweet solution as well. Following are some simple and effective methods for controlling ants.

~ Make a moat on the feeder's suspending wire. Punch a hole in a jar lid or bottle cap and place the cap on the wire about halfway down. Use a bit of silicone glue underneath the cap to hold it in place and make it waterproof. Just fill the cap with water (or even mentholated rub) and you have a barrier moat for your feeder.

~ A sticky string is another option. Tie a strong piece of string to the feeder's suspending wire, so that when the feeder is hung it will hang down an extra four or five inches. After you hang the feeder, smear Tanglefoot (which you can buy at any garden shop) on the string. It is extremely sticky, so be careful.

~ A hot chile solution, such as hot sauce or cayenne pepper, can also be applied to the suspending string to help keep ants away.

~ Oil of eucalyptus applied to a suspending string is also an excellent way of repelling ants. If you can't find oil of eucalyptus, use metholated rub instead.

LADYBUGS (LADYBIRD BEETLES)

Who doesn't know of this aphid-loving beetle, which children tell to "fly away home"? To most gardeners, this little dynamo is surely worth its weight in gold (or at least fertilizer!).

Aphid annihilator

Ladybird beetles belong to the beetle family *Coccinellidae*. Except for two species, the Mexican bean beetle and the squash beetle, all the members of this group are beneficial. This well-known family consists of insects that are small, oval, well-rounded, and often brightly colored. Most of us are familiar with the ladybug that is red with black spots and a black head, but many others come in various shades of orange, brown, yellow, or solid black. These can have various numbers of spots or be spotless, and are all separate species.

Both the adult and the larval forms of the ladybird beetle will feed together on a colony of aphids. The larval form, called aphid lions, usually devours more aphids than the adults because adults will also eat nectar and pollen from plants. Since a single female beetle can lay up to 1000 eggs in her life span, you can see exactly how necessary ladybird beetles are to the control of aphids.

Ladybird beetles eat not only aphids, but other pest insects as well. One well-known species, called the mealybug destroyer, does a great job of controlling mealybugs and scale insects.

Welcoming a friend

Nursery rhymes notwithstanding, nothing is more frustrating than bringing home a container of ladybugs for your garden and watching them fly away when you release them. Release your new ladybugs at dusk and they'll surely stay at least until morning. But if you want them to stay longer than that, first do a bit of investigation in your yard. Check to see if ladybugs are hanging around a particular plant. Many prefer leafy plants to hide in. If you *do* notice a favored plant, take note and plant more of these to attract native ladybird beetles to your yard. Next look for plants and shrubs with aphids on them. The beetles will not hang around if there is no food for them or their young. If you decide to buy extra beetles, first check to make sure that the species you are buying is right for your pest problem.

LIZARDS

Many people find lizards almost as repulsive as snakes. But lizards, just like snakes, are great predators. No self-respecting lizard could pass up a tasty insect meal. So before you swoosh that lizard away from your garden, encourage him to hang around for a meal.

The benefits of having a lizard around

Most lizards are diurnal, meaning they are awake in the daytime and asleep at night. Many of our most dreaded pests are also diurnal, so try using the following tricks to encourage that lizard you saw prowling around your garden to look for a meal when pests are most active.

Small clay pots turned upside down, or an old wooden box in the corner of your yard, can provide a good hiding place for a lizard. However, most lizards prefer to live in grassy cover, and well-manicured yards don't provide much shelter for them. A small "wild" patch of herbs or flowers will give lizards the shelter they need. Lizards also use secluded areas to wait for their prey. Rock walls are a favorite spot. They provide cover and a warm place to bask.

If you are lucky enough to have an alligator lizard in your yard, you probably don't have any black widow spiders. Alligator lizards will climb bushes and shrubs, or prowl dark basements and garages, in search of this delicious prey. In the absence of black widows, this lizard is also known to feed on almost any small animal that it can catch and swallow.

The lives of lizards

Lizards belong to the largest living group of reptiles and date back to the Triassic Period. There are 115 different species of lizards in North America and 3,000 species worldwide.

Lizards can be found in many shapes, sizes, and colors. Some lizards don't even look like lizards, but instead look like snakes. The only way to tell a legless lizard from a snake is to look at its eyes. Legless lizards have movable eyelids, while snakes do not.

Many people confuse lizards with salamanders. Salamanders are amphibians and have moist skin, no scales, no claws, and spend part of their lives (the egg stage) in water. Lizards, on the other hand, have scales and claws, and they lay eggs on land. Salamanders, like lizards, are carnivores that are great to have around.

As you've probably noticed, lizards vary greatly in size. The smallest lizard is a gecko that is less that 3 inches long when grown, and the largest is the Komodo dragon, from a small island in Indonesia, which can reach a length of 10 feet and weigh up to 300 pounds.

Not all lizards are strictly meat eaters. Many lizards will also eat plants, but damage done by lizards is usually minimal, if it happens at all.

When the weather gets cold, lizards don't congregate in dens, as many snakes do. Instead they usually hibernate alone in cracks and crevices. In the spring you will again see the lizards sunning themselves on rocks and fences.

There are only two lizards that are venomous—the gila monster of the southwestern U.S. and Mexico's beaded lizard. They do not have fangs, as snakes do, but instead have grooves in their back teeth. When venomous lizards bite, they hold on until the venom runs down the grooves in their teeth and into the wound. They are pretty slow moving and generally do not pose much danger to man.

NEMATODES

 Nematodes are minute nonsegmented worms that are pointed on both ends. Many nematodes are parasitic and, when added to the soil, will seek out and destroy pests, including fleas, cutworms, and beetle grubs. However, some nematodes are also plant parasites that cause plant diseases.

Insect assassins

As beneficial as some nematodes are, there are others that are equally destructive. Nematodes that are plant parasites attack plant roots, causing damage to the root, which prevents the plant from getting the water and nutrients it needs to grow. Don't be surprised if you go to a nursery looking for beneficial nematodes and get surprised looks in return. Some plant nematodes are major pests, and news of beneficial nematodes is slow to circulate.

Certain nematode species also are parasitic to animals. Canine heartworms, hookworms, and pinworms are a few common animal nematode parasites.

Beneficial nematodes are those that are known to attack specific organisms. The nematode that is specific for fleas only attacks fleas, so you don't have to worry that it will attack something else in your garden. It has been estimated that soil-dwelling nematodes have the potential to kill more than 400 different kinds of borer and soil-dwelling pests.

When a nematode enters a host, it releases a bacterium that slowly kills the host. The nematode needs the host to complete its life cycle. The offspring that are produced then go out and search for a new host. If all the host species are gone, the nematodes will die.

The common species of nematodes commercially sold for garden application, *Sc (Steinernema carpocapsae)* and *Hb (Hererorhabditis bacteriophora)*, are usually available in the spring. There are various strains of each and your local nursery personnel should know which ones are effective in your area and for your problem. The nematodes that target fleas can also be found in many pet supply outlets.

Nematodes are most effective in the first two to three weeks after application. The nematodes will continue to control pests after that, but they need a moist soil environment in which to live, so reapplication may be necessary if the soil dries out too much and pests are still present.

Follow directions carefully when applying the nematodes to the soil. You don't want to expose them to direct sunlight, so it's best to apply them in the late evening after the soil has been moistened. This gives the nematodes the best chance to get into the soil and do the job you want them to do. Also, try not to mix different types of nematodes together in the same area at the same time. Some nematode species don't live well together.

PARASITIC WASPS

Most parasitic wasps are quite tiny and therefore are generally not noticed by humans, but the job they do killing pests is nothing less than monumental.

Small wonders

The wasp does its killing by laying its eggs on the eggs and larvae of a target host. The eggs of the wasp hatch and start feeding on the host. Some parasitic wasp larvae feed on the outside of the host, while others bore into the host and feed from the inside. The host slowly dies as the immature larval wasp matures.

Most parasitic wasps belong to one of these insect superfamilies: *Ichnumonoidea, Bracondidae, Chalcidoidea,* and *Proctotrupoidea.*

Many of these tiny wasps are commercially available. They are usually shipped as pupae in parasitized hosts, and are ready to be distributed among your plants, where they will emerge as adults and search for hosts on which to lay their eggs.

Some of the more important parasitic wasps are:

~ The whitefly parasite (*Encarsia formosa*) lays its eggs in the scale-like nymph stage of the whitefly, causing the scale to blacken as the wasps develop and eat the host from the inside. It is recommended that you release these wasps in warm weather, at a rate of two to five wasps per square foot of garden. It's best to release the wasps weekly over a two-month period.

~ Trichogramma wasps are extremely tiny wasps that are of great benefit to the gardener. One species, *Trichogramma pretiosum*, will seek out and parasitize the eggs of about 200 different kinds of butterflies and moths. Other species of trichogramma wasps are a bit more specific in their selection of hosts. Most experts recommend one wasp for every foot of garden. It is best to release the wasps at the time when most host species lay their eggs. Your neighborhood nursery or county agriculture department will have the correct information for your area.

~ The pedio wasp (*Pediobius foveolatus*), or bean beetle parasite, is an excellent addition in the fight against Mexican bean beetles. This wasp targets the beetle's larval stage.

Most of the parasitic wasps that are commercially available will be found for sale at nurseries and garden supply outlets, or you can buy them directly from a supplier. We've listed only a few examples of the many pest species that are targeted by parasitic wasps. Directions for best results usually come with the purchased wasps, but you should also ask other gardeners or professionals in your area which wasps work best for them, and under what conditions.

A list of commercial suppliers dealing in beneficial insects can be found in the buying guide in the back of this book.

PRAYING MANTISES

Generally, when people think of insects that are great to have around the garden, they think of the praying mantis. Those large, green, fascinating insects seem to understand every word you say to them. (Or at least they turn their heads like they're listening!)

His benefits are just so-so

Unfortunately, the lovely insect that we have come to admire for its beneficial qualities only rates a poor to average in pest control. They are indeed predators, but they'll eat any insect they find, whether that insect is beneficial or a pest. (They'll even eat each other.) All an insect has to do is pass within reach to become the mantis' lunch.

Many gardeners have purchased praying mantises and introduced them into their gardens. They usually arrive as egg cases, and the hope is that the praying mantises will hatch and keep pest populations down. Unfortunately, the nymphs have a low survival rate and few develop into adults.

Praying or preying?

Praying mantises got their name from the way they wait for their prey. Because they sit perfectly still with their front legs upraised, people thought they looked like they were praying.

Praying mantises belong to the insect family *Mantidae* and are cousins of the walking sticks and crickets. These slow-moving insects are usually green to brown in color and can range up to 5 inches in length, though in the U.S. the average length is 2 to 3 inches. Mantises are chiefly tropical insects, but they have been successfully introduced to cooler climates.

The distinctive front legs of the mantis possess strong spines that can snap back firmly to hold its prey. The mantis is a voracious eater, and the female will consume the male after mating. Interestingly, the mantis is the only insect that can turn its head and look backwards. Snakeflies can also turn their heads but can't look backwards. Other insects must turn their entire bodies to look behind them.

Mantises overwinter as eggs, with 200 or more packed in an egg case (*ootheca*) that is laid in the grass or on twigs. The young hatch in early summer and start looking for anything to eat, usually their own brothers and sisters. Mantises, which have only one generation per year, usually reach full maturity in early fall.

ROBBER FLIES

 Have you ever been out in your yard and seen a large bee swoop out of nowhere, grab another insect, and fly off? No, you weren't seeing things. Some robber flies look like bees, and most prey on other insects.

A wolf in sheep's clothing

What better way to get close to your prey than by appearing to be a harmless neighbor? That's just what robber flies love to do. They lie in wait, and then dart out and grab their victims in midair, hence their name.

Robber flies belong to the fly family *Asilidae*, which has over 850 different North American species. They are predaceous in both the larval form and the adult form. As larvae, they live underground or in decaying wood and feed primarily on the eggs and larvae of beetles and other insects. It's as adults that robber flies do their best insect control. They will feed on just about any insect they can catch, from bees to dragonflies.

Robber flies have many guises. They range from ¼ to 1¼ inches in length and resemble flies, bees, and wasps. All of them have bulging eyes with a dent in between, two wings (true bees have four wings), antennae that project prominently forward, and a long proboscis, which they use to stab their victims. Most robber flies have a very long and pointed abdomen, but this isn't seen in the species of robber flies that resemble bees. They also make a very loud buzzing sound when they fly, sounding almost like a bee that needs a tune-up!

Inviting them home

Good news—you really don't have to do anything special to encourage robber flies to visit your garden. If you have insects in your yard, then chances are you'll have robber flies looking for a free meal.

Robber flies are especially good at making meals of flying insects. They are fast fliers and prefer to catch their prey on the wing. Sometimes the robber fly will sit motionless in a tall plant or tree and wait for a victim to fly into range. The robber fly will then dart out and grab the insect with its long legs, which are specially designed with spurs on the inside to hold the prey. These flies will actually attack insects as large as or sometimes even larger than themselves. Robber flies can be found in just about any habitat, even at the tops of giant sequoia trees. Because of their great flying skills, you probably won't see robber flies stopping to eat aphids from a leaf—even though many of us wish they would!

TOADS AND FROGS

Last time your children brought you a toad they found in your yard, what did you do? Have them drop it over the fence into your neighbor's yard? Next time, think twice, because that little toad is a giant asset to your garden.

Calling all toads (and frogs)

Toads and frogs are truly insect-eating machines. No insect is immune from the lightning-fast tongues of these amphibians. One toad or frog in your garden can go a long way toward keeping insects under control.

> One lowly toad can eat between 10,000 and 20,000 slugs, flies, grubs, cutworms, or grasshoppers (or any other insect you can name) per year!

A toad isn't just a sometime carnivore. Some predators will start nibbling on your garden vegetables when their favorite food supply is exhausted, but toads won't. If the toad's food supply disappears (and it usually doesn't), the toad will move on and look for insects elsewhere. But with a bit of planning, you can make toads, and even frogs, permanent guests in your yard.

All amphibians need water to complete their life cycles. Frogs are much more dependent on water than toads are and will require a garden pond to take up residency in your yard. A toad, however, will survive nicely with some shelter and a large clay saucer full of water. The shelter can be made of anything that will provide a fairly damp environment. A small cave in a rock garden (or just a broken clay pot turned upside down) can provide an excellent home for a toad. Just make sure the opening is big enough for the toad and sheltered from the wind.

Toads and frogs are very susceptible to pesticide poisoning, so be extremely careful with any toxic products near the toad's or frog's home or pond.

Don't kiss too many frogs

An old wives' tale tells of getting warts from handling frogs and toads. Most people know this isn't true, but they don't know that some toads and frogs secrete a toxin from their skin which can be very irritating.

BENEFICIAL PLANTS AND ALL-PURPOSE REPELLENTS

INSECT-REPELLING PLANTS

 Our ancestors routinely used companion plants for more effective gardening. Before the invention of chemical pesticides, the art of using companion plants to confuse, repel, or attract insects was relied upon for successful food production. Most gardeners today know very little of the garden practices of long ago, and some of this lost knowledge could be beneficial to both the gardener and the environment.

The benefits of companion plants become obvious when you see the number of pests decrease, but the ways in which companion plants keep pests away are as varied as the plants themselves. Following are some of the ways companion plantings protect your garden vegetables:

~ By producing an odor that masks or hides your garden from a pest

~ By producing an odor that repels a pest

~ As a trap plant that attracts the pest, so it can be easily removed from your garden

~ As a perfect breeding ground for beneficial insects, by providing food and/or shelter

Ornamental flowers and garden plants

Many of us are familiar with the repellent quality of marigolds, and some of us have even tried them in our gardens just to see if they really work. Beneficial insects need a constant food source in your garden, and many flowering plants, including marigolds, produce numerous flowers rich in pollen and nectar for the entire growing season. Various other flowers and garden plants have also been found to be helpful to the gardener, and many of these have been mentioned in other sections of this book. Here are some popular companion plantings you can try.

~ Grown with carrots, onions can help control destructive nematodes.

~ Growing horseradish with potatoes helps repel Colorado potato beetles.

~ Catnip planted near eggplant deters flea beetles.

~ Planting tomatoes or parsley with asparagus helps control asparagus beetles.

~ Parsley gone to flower makes a great attractant and food source for the beneficial braconid wasp.

~ Nasturtiums planted as a border can help deter whiteflies and squash bugs.

~ Nasturtiums are a favorite of aphids, and planting them near your garden will provide a trap plant for aphids.

~ Allow a few of your radishes or broccoli to go to flower— these blossoms make a great attractant for many beneficial insects.

~ Our friend the marigold, planted in vegetable gardens, produces a scent that repels many garden pests. Some marigolds, like the beautiful lemon-scented marigold, are loved by beneficial insects.

~ Mint is said to repel mosquitoes and also produces an odor that many cabbage pests and aphids dislike.

~ Spearmint is a favorite of beneficial insects.

~ Rue, carefully planted (some people are allergic to it), is known to repel Japanese beetles.

~ Many beneficial insects love buckwheat, so plant some if you have the room.

~ Tansy has a long history of repelling cucumber beetles, Japanese beetles, squash beetles, and even ants. However, only use tansy in a garden without cabbage, since cabbage worms love it. Tansy is also a favorite of many beneficial insects.

~ Cosmos planted around the garden can attract many beneficial insects.

~ Early-flowering plants such as gazanias and calendulas will help beneficials get established in your garden early, so they'll be ready for any pests that try to move in.

~ Yarrow produces a lot of pollen and nectar, and is prized by many beneficials, such as bees and wasps.

~ Ladybird beetles love morning glory and goldenrod.

~ Many species of candytuft will attract beneficial syrphid flies.

Herbs

Herb planting to control unwanted pests has an extra advantage, because when it's time to harvest the crop you've protected with the herbs, you can harvest the herbs too. They can be used fresh in cooking or dried for later use. Here are some excellent companion plantings using herbs.

~ Planting basil alongside your tomatoes helps control tomato hornworms.

~ Thyme planted with cabbage helps control flea beetles, cabbage worms, and white cabbage butterflies.

~ Dill is great to plant not only for its herb quality, but because beneficial insects like it for its pollen and nectar.

~ Fennel is a favorite of many beneficials.

~ Anise planted in your yard will give off a lovely licorice smell (and attract parasitic wasps, too).

ANIMAL-REPELLING PLANTS

Gopher Plants

Maybe you've heard of this wonderful plant, which, when planted in and around a garden, repels gophers and other animals like mad. What is it, and how does it work?

PLANTS TO THE RESCUE The gopher or mole plant (*Euphorbia lathyris*) is a member of a very diverse group of plants. Euphorbias can be shrubs, perennials, biennials, annuals, or succulents. Most have milky sap that is very unpleasant in taste and odor. Some are poisonous and quite irritating to the skin. Most euphorbia flowers are a group of colored bracts, not true flowers. The true flowers are usually inside the bracts and are very inconspicuous.

Legend claims that the gopher plant's sap is so poisonous and irritating that gophers and moles can't stand to be anywhere near it. However, test trials indicate mixed results from the plant. But if you happen to be one of those for whom the plant works—that's great. Plant it around your garden for gopher protection. The sap is indeed poisonous, so be careful about planting it around small children and chewing pets.

GOPHER IT! The gopher plant, which grows well from seed, should be planted in an area that gets full sun. The plant is a biennial and will reach its full height of five feet by the second year. It grows as a tall single stem with long, narrow pointed leaves growing at right angles to the stem. During the second year, it will set a cluster of yellow flowers at the top of the stem. When the flowers set seed, the plant will die. Most nurseries will either carry gopher plant seeds or can order them for you.

ALL-PURPOSE REPELLENTS

Chiles

Chiles can be one of a gardener's greatest allies. Depending on the type of pest that is bothering your garden, chiles prepared in many different forms can be just what the doctor ordered.

Chiles are members of the *Capsicum* plant family, which has over 200 different varieties. They have been traced as far back as 6200 B.C. in Peru. Christopher Columbus even got into the act when he first found chiles and thought they were peppers, hence the common name of chile peppers. But chiles are not peppers at all—true peppers are what we use in our pepper mills.

The use of chiles spread quickly through trade and now chiles are grown throughout the world. Not only are they used as food, flavoring, and medicine, but now we have discovered a new use for the chile—it's an all-purpose repellent!

When using chiles for repellents, you need to use "hot" chiles. Chiles are rated under a system called Scoville Heat Units. The higher the number in the rating system, the hotter the chile. For example, the common bell pepper rates 0, jalapeños rate 3,500 to 4,500 units, tabascos rate 30,000 to 50,000 units, and habaneros rate a whopping 200,000 to 300,000 units. The units rate the heat produced by the compound capsaicin, which is inside the ribs of the chile. Generally, the smaller the chile, the higher the heat units.

Chiles are easy to grow, and it's a good idea to grow a few plants for that special repellent cocktail you'll be making for the uninvited "guests" that keep dropping by. Chiles grow into nice bushy plants, usually 1½ to 2 feet tall. They look beautiful as a low hedge or in containers. Chile plants are easy to find in your local nursery, but if you are looking for a particularly hot variety, chances are you will have to order seeds. If your nursery can't order them for you, check out *The Whole Chile Pepper Book* by Dave DeWitt and Nancy Gerlach (Little, Brown and Company,

1990). It has lists of seed companies that sell seeds for the hottest chiles.

Chiles develop their hottest flavor when they are fully ripe, so don't be tempted to pick them early. Plant them in full sun to really bring out the flavor. A reminder: wear rubber gloves when picking and preparing the hottest chiles. If the capsaicin gets on your hands, you don't want to accidentally touch your eyes or nose.

O.K., now you've gotten your chiles ready for action. There are several ways to prepare them for use as repellents. In dry powder form, chiles can be sprinkled around areas where rabbits and small creatures are nibbling. You can discourage deer from chewing on small tree trunks by dabbing on a paste made of pureed chiles. (Freeze the extra paste for later use.)

A tea made of chiles can be sprayed on plants and vegetables as a repellent, but care should be taken to check sensitive plants for burning first. Also, remember to wash the vegetables before eating them, unless you like them chile-flavored. If you like, you can add other ingredients, such as garlic, to your tea as well (see page 111).

• Chile tea •

3 to 4 hot chiles, chopped (serranos and habaneros are good choices)

1 quart boiling water

Add the chopped chiles to the boiling water and let steep for 24 hours. Discard the chiles. The solution should be quite strong, so on delicate plants you may want to dilute it by adding another quart of water. Play with this recipe until you find the perfect strength, always remembering to start weak and gradually move to a stronger solution. If the spray doesn't stick well to the plants, add a couple of drops of liquid dish detergent.

Eucalyptus

Eucalyptus has become more and more popular as a medicinal remedy, and now it's known to be an excellent insect repellent as well. The pungent odor of eucalyptus has much the same effect as cedar—and who hasn't heard of lining a closet with cedar to repel moths?

A NEW OLD FRIEND Eucalyptus trees are a fairly new arrival to many mild climates, but they've been grown in California since 1856. Early on, the trees were mostly used for windbreaks, shade, and firewood. Their popularity has since grown, and now they are a favorite landscape tree in many states.

When you crush eucalyptus leaves in your hands, the wonderful smell of the tree is released. A mulch made from eucalyptus, when spread around your garden, is sure to stop quite a few insects as well as animals.

Shavings from the tree will work in Fido's bed just like cedar shavings do. If your area has an abundance of eucalyptus trees, you can save money by using eucalyptus shavings instead of buying expensive bagged cedar shavings.

If eucalyptus trees don't grow in your area, you can buy oil of eucalyptus at a health food store instead. The oil is a concentrated extract that can be diluted and sprayed on wood shavings for the same effect. The oil can also be used on a hummingbird feeder's string to deter ants from reaching the sugar solution.

Eucalyptus oil can be diluted to make an insect repellent. If you want to try it (and you don't mind smelling a bit like a eucalyptus tree), dilute the oil until there is just a faint odor of eucalyptus (try about ¼ teaspoon oil to 1 cup of water), and spray it on your skin. This repellent is said to work on fleas, ticks, chiggers, mosquitoes, and gnats as well. You may have to play with the amount of oil in the spray, adding more to keep those really pesky bugs away.

Now that you've made a spray that works for you, you can also spray it on your plants. No studies have been made to determine which garden insects it repels, but, given its reputation, it's worth a try. One way to use this spray is on the borders of fences and lawns. Because eucalyptus oil is a good flea repellent, it may keep neighborhood fleas from entering your yard.

You can also make eucalytus flea repellents for your pets. Dry eucalyptus leaves and crush them into a powder to use like flea powder, or make a eucalyptus spray flea repellent (see page 53).

Garlic

Garlic has long been known to have many beneficial qualities (besides warding off vampires) for both people and animals. It repels many of the major insect pests, especially aphids, and it has been shown to lessen the need for other control measures. Garlic is easy to grow, and mixed with your garden vegetables, it will afford them general insect protection. You will also have the benefit of harvesting a wonderful herb for cooking.

GROWING GARLIC Most gardeners plant garlic in the spring, when they plant their gardens, but in warm climates, fall plantings are not uncommon. Garlic can be grown from seeds or cloves. It does best in full sun but will do nicely on a window sill. Plant garlic cloves two inches deep and five inches apart in soil that drains well. It will sprout in ten to fourteen days and will require only water from then on to produce a bulb of good quality. Garlic is usually ready to harvest in about 120 days, but you can also leave it to reseed itself for the next year.

GARLIC AS A REPELLENT

~ Garlic planted close to roses has been shown to protect the bushes from black spot, a fungus disease.

~ As a companion crop, grown in rings around the desired crop, garlic has been particularly beneficial in repelling aphids from Brussels sprouts, cabbage, and cauliflower.

~ Feeding garlic to dogs is said to repel fleas. The recommended dose is one to two cloves a day, but it would be a good idea to adjust this amount depending on your dog's size. Parsley mixed with the garlic will help neutralize the garlic breath. (Parsley works for people, too!)

~ A garlic tea, sprayed on your plants, can provide protection from many insects, and even animals, which dislike the garlic's odor. Garlic spray has also been credited with eliminating fungus and mildew on plants.

FUN FACTS Garlic is thought to originate in Siberia. Marco Polo even wrote about garlic as a new discovery in cooking, recording what was possibly the first recipe in history to incorporate garlic.

Ancient Romans used garlic to increase their strength and courage. They also greatly prized it as a powerful aphrodisiac.

> **• Garlic tea •**
> 1 bulb of garlic (about 20 cloves), chopped
> 1 quart of hot water
> Place chopped garlic in the water and let steep for at least 24 hours. Strain and use.

Egyptians also held garlic in great esteem. The workers who built the great pyramids were given a daily ration of garlic, and the Egyptians used garlic as a major trade item. Cloves of garlic were even found in the tomb of King Tutankhamun.

Native Americans used garlic medicinally to treat stomachaches, headaches, coughs, and heart problems. There are also accounts of their use of garlic to treat insect and snake bites.

FOUR-LEGGED INTRUDERS

CATS AND DOGS

Most of us, at one time or another, have been faced with the problem of unwanted animals in our yards and gardens. Whether they're dogs, cats, or other animals, they come to our yards to dig, forage for food, deposit feces, or just make a mess.

Sending that animal on its way

Use negative reinforcement to discourage animals from visiting your property. If a yard smells bad to an animal, it will often pass it by. Make your yard or garden as unattractive as possible by offending the animal's sense of smell. Our chile-garlic and rotten egg repellents are sure to have those animals turning up their noses at your plants.

• Hot and garlicky repellent •

3-4 garlic cloves, crushed

3-4 hot chiles, chopped or puréed (habaneros work great)

$1/2$ teaspoon dishwasher detergent

3 gallons water

Mix all ingredients together and let steep for 24 hours. Dribble the mixture around your yard and garden.

Apply the chile-garlic mixture every few days for two to three weeks. The animals will hopefully find your property offensive for a long enough period of time that they'll get discouraged from using it. The rotten-smelling repellent should stay offensive to animals for about a week after applying, if the weather is dry.

Another way to keep dogs and cats or other animals out of desirable areas is to plant thorny bushes, such as pyracantha and barberry, around the edges of your yard. Where you don't want to plant hedges, just lay cuttings of the thorny bushes around the garden area to keep the animals out temporarily.

• **Rotten-smelling repellent** •

6 eggs, broken and beaten

6 oz. bottle of hot sauce (the hotter the better)

1 gallon of water

Place all ingredients in a large container with a tight-fitting lid. Shake until mixed and let sit one week. Spray or dribble the foul-smelling mixture around your garden or yard.

DEER

Who hasn't marveled at one time or another at the gracefulness of deer? Unfortunately for gardeners, these gentle creatures can decimate a garden in no time flat. They will eat just about anything you plant and will come back time after time once they know food is available at your place.

Discouraging the dear deer

If you're tired of feeding your entire garden to deer every year, the best defense is a good offense—an offensive smell, that is. Deer use their sense of smell to detect predators and dangerous situations, so targeting this sense is one of the best and easiest ways to discourage them. Smells that seem odd to them trigger their defense mechanism, causing them to flee.

Plant Protect Sticks, which clip onto plants and emit a garlic smell, can be purchased at your local nursery. Strong-smelling soap bars can also be quite effective at controlling deer. Drill holes in the bars and hang them around the edges of your garden or from the limbs of trees. Placing the bars no more than three feet apart will give the best control.

The smell of an animal's or person's hair will also deter deer. Place hair gathered from a pet groomer or hair stylist around the perimeter of prized plants, ringing the plant so that the deer encounters the hair before the branches or stems of the plant. Placing the hair around the base of the plant will usually provide little help if the plant is large.

Urine of other animals is another effective deer repellent. If you don't have a dog to do the job for you, find a friendly neighbor who will be happy to direct Fido to the right spots. Used cat litter sprinkled around the borders of your yard can also help send the deer away.

Many of the sprays and solutions used to deter other animals in this book will also work on deer. Any new smell that is unfamiliar to the deer will work. Baby powder, chile powder, or even clothes dryer sheets are worth a try when combating the destructive deer.

Keep in mind that deer are pretty clever animals; after a while, the new scent you are using to deter them will become familiar, and they will lose the desire to flee. You'll need to change or alternate the offensive smells in your yard to keep the deer wary. Keep track of which scents work and for how long, so you can use this information in planning your defense for the next year. However, in very severe conditions, like during droughts and floods, hungry deer will eat anything green no matter what it smells like. Another fact that should be noted: if your yard is especially tempting, with many of your local deer's favorite foods, offensive smells may not be enough of a deterrent.

You can, however, try making your plants also taste bad by spraying them with a bitter solution. Make your own bitter sprays with horseradish, hot chiles, or vinegar mixed with water, or try using a commercial bitter apple spray. (Your homemade solution should be strong enough to be pretty bitter to your taste buds.) Unfortunately, these sprays only work when the deer starts eating your plants, so some damage will occur using this method. Don't forget to wash the bitter solutions off plants you plan to eat, or you will have the same reaction as the deer.

Finally, if all else fails (and sometimes it does), fencing and barriers may be the only ways to keep your garden free of deer. Because deer are fairly large, a good fence should be at least eight feet high. Wire mesh placed around and over plants will also be quite effective.

Getting to know the real deer

Deer are members of the mammal family *Cervidae*, which also includes moose, elk, and caribou. The moose is the largest of the deer species, weighing up to 1,200 pounds. Most deer species average around 400 pounds in weight.

All deer leave a split-hoof imprint that looks like two toes. The males have antlers that they shed every year, and in some species, the females will also have antlers. Deer, which are cud-chewing herbivores, lack top front teeth—and you have to wonder how they eat without them. They can eat great quantities of food and can completely strip trees and shrubs in times of famine.

Female deer become sexually mature at about age 1½ and males at about age 2½. In late summer, the rutting (breeding) season begins for most species. After breeding, females usually give birth to a fawn in late spring. One fawn is normally born, but twins are not uncommon.

GOPHERS

Fan-shaped mounds of dirt are appearing in your yard and garden. You've even noticed whole plants missing. Sounds like you may be a victim of the dreaded gopher.

Going after the gopher

People have tried many methods to rid their yards of gophers. Some are more successful than others, depending on the conditions of one's yard. One secret is to start treatment immediately upon seeing the first signs of gophers, before the tunneling is extensive and much harder to treat. Gophers are opportunistic and will take over an abandoned burrow if they can. Often just one remedy is not enough to deter gophers, so try various combinations of the following deterrents to find the right solution for you.

~ Plant gopher plants (*Euphorbia lathyrus*), which you can find at your local nursery, two to three feet apart around your prized garden. Gophers dislike this plant and hopefully will avoid it. (See page 104.)

~ Other plants also known to deter gophers are daffodils and castor bean plants. Castor bean plants are extremely poisonous and probably should not be planted where pets or children can get near them.

~ Placing newspapers around your plants and yard is an old trick that may keep a gopher from surfacing. However, it doesn't keep a gopher from tunneling under your plants and eating the roots!

~ Dumping used kitty litter, dog droppings, or hair clippings into the gopher's tunnel may convince it there's a predator nearby and encourage it to leave. This is a good method to try in a small yard or garden. You might have to repeat this method a few times to prove to the gopher that a predator is around.

~ Scaring gophers away is a popular method; many people swear by whirligigs or pinwheels placed around their yards. It is believed the vibrations produced by these devices annoy or scare the gophers and force them to find a new home elsewhere. Some ultrasonic devices now sold for this very purpose claim to protect an area from rodents (including gophers) for up to 1000 square yards.

~ Sound deterrents, which work along the same lines as whirligigs, may also help. Try leaving empty soda bottles around your yard, anchored or partially buried for best results. The noise produced when the wind passes over the bottles will scare away many forms of wildlife.

~ Probably the best way to protect your garden from gophers is to line your garden beds both on the sides and on the bottom with chicken wire. This requires a lot of work to sink the wire 'basket' at least eighteen to twenty-four inches deep. Be sure to connect the sides and bottom of the basket securely to prevent any holes that the gopher might find. This method works best for raised-bed gardens.

~ While the gopher is on the surface, it is an easy target for many predators, including cats, owls, and foxes. However, few predators, except for snakes and some members of the weasel family, will tackle the territorial gopher down in its burrow. Although most people don't want weasels or snakes in their yards either, a large king snake is a predator that most gardeners should be happy to have around. They will not only eat any rodent, but will also eat rattlesnakes.

~ Packing dry ice in the tunnel in high concentrations will suffocate the gopher. This method works best when the tunnels aren't very extensive. At the very least, it will send the gopher elsewhere for the moment.

~ The old method of placing a hose down the gopher's hole to flush it out is still effective, especially if the gopher's tunneling system is small. Do this in the morning and evening when the gopher is most active. Use barbecue tongs to catch the gopher if it appears from the flooded hole. Drop the gopher in a bucket and dispatch as you please.

~ The old-fashioned gopher trap available at garden and home centers is still popular with many people.

A gopher's lonely life

There are thirty-three different species of gophers, but the species with which most people are familiar, and with which they have the most difficulty, is the pocket gopher. Pocket gophers were named for the fur-lined pouches or pockets inside their cheeks, which they use to carry food. Like all gophers, pocket gophers are rodents. They are varying shades of brown, about 5 to 9 inches long, with short legs and long curved claws designed for digging.

Most of the time gophers are loners; they are very protective of their tunnels and will defend them against invaders. One gopher can have an elaborate tunnel system that can cover about 700 square yards of ground. The tunneling can be deep or shallow, and generally there is one main tunnel with many side tunnels. Gophers, which are great soil cultivators and aerators, prefer soft soils with good drainage but can also be found elsewhere.

Gophers generally give birth to litters of four offspring in the spring. Sometimes, in warm climates, gopher females will have two litters in a season. Gophers do not hibernate (as ground squirrels do) and can feed day and night all year round. As they tunnel, they will feed on any delicious roots they find. The babies are usually pushed out of the mother's burrow after six weeks to find their own territory.

GROUND SQUIRRELS

Holes without mounds of dirt around them have started appearing in your yard. Nearly every plant has been nibbled on, and some—especially fruits, seeds, and berries—have been eaten completely. Yes, the cute little brown squirrels you see scurrying about are eating their way through your garden and yard.

Squirrel, squirrel go away

Like gophers, ground squirrels are very difficult to control once they have decided your yard is the perfect habitat. The trial and error method is the best approach for controlling them. If one remedy doesn't work, try another, or even mix remedies to find the perfect combination for your yard. The following are a few methods that have worked under a variety of conditions.

Try trapping them using a Havaheart live trap baited with nuts, fruit, or peanut butter. This can be an ongoing battle, but it works! Check to see if your local animal control will pick up the animals for you, and what the laws are concerning relocating the squirrels if you catch one. Always wear gloves and *never* handle a ground squirrel. Some ground squirrels are known to carry the fleas that can transmit Rocky Mountain spotted fever. Fortunately, no cases of the fever have been reported in recent years.

Squirrels are known to dislike plants sprayed with a chile pepper solution, so try making your own chile spray to deter them. Keep in mind that you may have to play with the amount of chiles (some are stronger than others) to get the perfect concentration to do the job.

• Squirrel pepper spray •

4 hot chiles (habanero, jalapeño, etc.)

3 gallons water

1 teaspoon dishwashing liquid

Puree the peppers with some of the water. Strain and discard the peppers. Add the rest of the water to the pepper solution. Add the dishwashing liquid. Spray around plants (but check for burning before spraying directly on plants).

Rototilling or turning over the soil regularly will destroy the squirrel's burrows. An extra deterrent is to rototill dog or cat droppings into the burrows. If the burrows are deep or in a place where you can't turn the soil over, then pack the burrow holes with the droppings. The squirrels will think a predator is nearby and will hopefully find a new home elsewhere.

Grapes and other hanging fruit are a perfect treat for squirrels. Try tying brown paper bags over low-hanging fruit to deter them. (This trick keeps birds from eating your fruit too.)

Squirrels love freshly planted seeds, so try placing chicken wire over beds to discourage squirrels from digging. Anchor the wire down, or the squirrels will just go under it.

Flat metal bands, or metal bands that are flared at the bottom, will help prevent squirrels from climbing into trees. Be sure to place the bands, which should be about twelve inches wide, high enough up the tree trunks so the squirrels can't jump over them.

Ground squirrels are a favorite prey of snakes. If you find a king snake or gopher snake in your yard, send it down one of the holes. The squirrels will leave immediately! (Hopefully never to return.)

One wild remedy suggests depositing male human urine in the squirrel's hole to send those squirrels packing.

Destructive diggers

Ground squirrels, which are a major pest problem, belong to the rodent family *Sciuridae*, which also includes tree squirrels and chipmunks. These digging rodents have cost taxpayers millions of dollars in damage to roadways, airport runways, and flood control levees. They weaken structures by undermining them, forcing replacement. The eradication measures necessary to get rid of the squirrels themselves drive the costs up even more. This damage is on top of the damage squirrels do to crops and gardens.

Ground squirrels are fairly large rodents, ranging in size from 9 to 11 inches, not including the tail, which can be another 5 to 9 inches long. They can weigh between 1 and 2.2 pounds. Unlike most squirrels, ground squirrels live in colonies. They usually have two litters each year, averaging seven young per litter. The babies are born in the spring and summer months and the young usually stay with the parents for about ten weeks. Squirrels and chipmunks usually hibernate, but in very warm regions they may skip the hibernation and feed all year round.

The burrows of ground squirrels are sometimes very elaborate, with secret entrances. Most squirrels are active during the day, foraging for food or working on their burrows. Squirrels will dig out specific chambers in their burrows, using some for storage and others for nesting. Usually there will be a network of paths between the entrance holes on the surface, so the squirrel is never far from a hole. In the winter, if it is cold enough for the squirrels to hibernate, they will close up the entrance holes with plant material.

MOLES

Oh, no—you've found signs of tunneling just under the surface in your garden or yard. You might have even found some dirt pushed to the surface but no exit hole. Gophers again? Actually, it sounds like you probably have a mole.

Mole holes

First, you need to determine which tunnels are active and which ones are just for foraging. Step on and press down all the tunnels (sometimes they look like ridges) in your yard. The mole will repair the main tunnels. Moles can dig about 200 feet per day if necessary, in search of insects.

• Mole Repellent •

2 tablespoons castor oil

1 tablespoon liquid dish-washing detergent

1 gallon water

Mix all ingredients together, and wet down the mole's tunnels with the solution. (This should send the mole packing.)

There are several strategies that may help you rid yourself of this subterranean dweller. Because moles are very sensitive to ground vibrations, the whirligigs and vibration-producing products mentioned on page 115 may help deter them. Placing dog or cat droppings in the tunnels may convince a mole that a predator is nearby, causing it to leave. Also, moles dislike very wet soils, so soaking their tunnels may also deter them.

Moles are known to dislike castor-bean plants, which are very poisonous and should only be planted with extreme caution. However, a spray made out of castor oil may also discourage a mole.

Cats have taken their toll on moles, and moles definitely try to avoid these predators. However, cats will often carry home a mole and refuse to eat it. It is thought the mole's musty odor makes it an unappetizing catch.

Insect eaters

Unlike gophers, moles are not rodents. They belong to the mammal order *Insectovora*, which gives you a clue to their habits.

Moles eat insects, grubs, and worms, but not plants. Moles won't eat your garden, but their tunneling activities in search of insects and worms can certainly make a mess of your yard. Many people feel a mole's beneficial role as a natural soil aerator outweighs any damage they do. (These people usually don't have moles in their backyards!)

Moles range in size from 2½ to 6 inches in length, with short tails. They are usually brown to black in color and have very broad front feet, which they use to swim through the soil. Their eyes are very small (about the size of a pinhead), and they have no external ears. Moles generally have one litter of four young per year, usually in the spring. The young are independent in about a month.

Moles are very territorial and are active both day and night. They are in constant search of food and prefer living in soft soils. You usually will not see a mole in extremely dry or wet soil, or where there are a lot of rocks. Because of their need to consume large quantities of insects, it is estimated that only two or three moles can survive per acre.

Opossums

Opossums, those large and unique-looking creatures, have decided your yard is a diner's delight and are proceeding to eat everything (and we do mean everything) in sight. No matter how many times you scare them away, they keep coming back. Can they really be that smart?

Smarter than they look

Opossums are good climbers and will climb most fences. Barriers, electric wires on tops of fences, and metal strips on fences (which keep the opossum from getting a grip) can help deter them. Despite their appearance, opossums are fairly intelligent and will usually find a way around or under the barriers. They can be pretty persistent at times.

Opossums are scavengers looking for anything to eat. The more accessible the food, the better. Opossums have been seen eating road kills, pet food left out overnight, mice, and just about any garden plant. Their front paws are very human-like, and when they pick up something to eat, they look like Bugs Bunny eating a carrot. Opossums are very fond of fruit, so ripe fruit, especially grapes, makes an excellent bait.

Trash cans are a favorite target, as are compost piles. The smell of ripe trash can drive an opossum into a feeding frenzy! You can use this knowledge to trap an unwanted opossum. Place an empty trash can next to a fence or porch where the opossum can easily jump down on it. Next place the trash can lid upside down and tilted so it will turn if pushed. Put a favorite opossum food, like grapes or bacon, on the tilted lid on the low side. When the opossum jumps onto the lid for the food, the lid will turn over quickly, dropping the opossum into the trash can. Now he can be relocated to the back country, far away from your garden. Remember to check local laws before relocating the opossum.

Commercial Havaheart live traps also work quite well for capturing opossums. You can usually rent these from your local animal shelter or feed store. Remember to wear gloves when transporting any wild animal. Even with the opossum's easy-going nature, and its habit of playing dead when truly frightened, it will bite if threatened. Opossums have fifty teeth, more than any other mammal, and they are all sharp.

Playing dead—a way of life

Opossums are frequently called possums, but true possums are a different animal that lives in Australia. The common opossum (*Didelphis virginiana*) is the only North American marsupial. Their bodies average 15 to 20 inches in length, with an additional 9 to 20 inches for their prehensile tail, and they can weigh between 9 and 13 pounds. Opossums are nocturnal and usually find a nice place under a deck or porch to sleep during the day. Opossums can have up to fourteen young in a litter, but ten offspring per litter is more common. Females usually have two litters per year. The young are born after only thirteen days of gestation and stay with the female for about two months. The average life span of an opossum is seven years, so you may find the same opossum back in your yard, year after year after year.

In many large cities, opossums are becoming so common that they are being considered pests, and animal shelters are being asked to control these animals. Because many cities do not have the funds to do such a job, homeowners have often had to find ways to deal with the persistent opossum on their own.

Q: Why did the chicken cross the road?

A: To prove to the opossum that it can be done.

The point of this riddle is that opossums are slow *and* have poor eyesight—a deadly combination when crossing busy streets. Despite this disadvantage, opossums are one of a handful of species that are flourishing near mankind.

RABBITS

Your garden looked great when you retired for the evening, but by the time you awakened, rows of seedling vegetables had been chewed to the ground. Small holes dug under your fence and telltale footprints point to a bunny attack. Those cute little rabbits can practically eat their weight in your garden produce in one night!

Keeping those bunnies away

Cages placed around young seedlings have long been used to deter hungry rabbits, and are still an excellent method of exclusion. Old milk cartons, strawberry baskets, and wire all make good cages. In areas of heavy rabbit infestation, the cages may need to be stronger and completely cover desired crops. Check the cages to be sure they are securely anchored so the bunnies don't go under the cage and defeat your effort.

Use the rabbit's keen nose against him and convince him a predator is

---

• Rabbit repellent •

4 cloves garlic

2 cups hot water

1 teaspoon fish emulsion

Steep the garlic in the hot water. When cool, discard the garlic and add fish emulsion.

To use, dilute 1 tablespoon of this mixture into 1 cup of water and spray around your garden plants, especially lettuce.

---

near by placing dog hair or dog droppings around the plants in your garden or along the fence. You can also make a rabbit repellent spray. Even if it doesn't keep the bunnies away, it will make a great plant fertilizer.

A product called Plant Protect Sticks, available at nurseries, claims to repel bunnies (and deer too) with a garlic odor. The sticks resemble small writing pens that clip onto the ends of plants. When the seal is broken, the stick emits the offensive scent.

Another anti-rabbit tactic is to sprinkle blood meal (available at places that sell organic fertilizer) around your yard. The smell of blood will repel the bunnies. In addition to ridding your yard of rabbits, blood meal is a great plant fertilizer and can be sprinkled around most plants. However, be sure to water throughly after applying the blood meal or it could burn your lawn or plants.

Several common treatments for repelling rabbits require making the plants they're after taste bad. Sprinkling the plants with red pepper powder, sulfur, or lime is said to leave a bitter taste in rabbits' mouths. Check your plants for burning, especially if you use the sulfur. The following are several other solutions that can serve the same purpose. Mix ingredients well and spray directly on the leaves of your plants, checking for burning as usual.

~ 1 teaspoon Lysol in 1 gallon water

~ 3 ounces Epsom salts in 1 gallon water

~ 1 ounce Black Leaf 40 in 1 gallon water

Trapping out rabbits is fairly easy with a Havaheart live trap. Place the trap near your garden, or, if you know how the rabbits are getting in, by the entrance hole to your yard. Bait with their favorite garden plant, alfalfa, or fruit.

The life of Peter Cottontail

Rabbits are timid creatures that are generally gray or brown in color. They usually come out in the late evening and early morning to forage for food, but some of the fifteen common American species of rabbits and hares are active during the day. They prefer young plants or the tender ends of bushes and shrubs.

Rabbits are not rodents, as many people believe, but belong to the order *Lagomorpha*. Like rodents, rabbits possess two large front incisor teeth but, unlike rodents, rabbits also have a smaller pair of incisors directly behind the front two.

The sheer number of rabbits is the biggest problem for most gardeners. Rabbits do indeed breed prolifically, with rabbit litters averaging four to eight young. A female rabbit can easily have six litters a year. The high breeding rate is necessary because rabbits are a major prey species and it is estimated that only about one percent of wild rabbits survive three years.

SKUNKS

 Skunks are digging up your lawn and raiding your yard. No way are you going outside to chase them away. Yelling at the varmints from your upstairs window hasn't scared them off either. What can you do?

Solving a smelly problem

A two-foot-high wire fence around your garden is a good start in keeping unwanted skunks out. However, skunks are pretty resourceful, and this may not be enough of a deterrent. Laying chicken wire around your garden or on top of your lawn will slow down most skunks. But don't anchor the wire down tightly—leave some small waves in it, because skunks don't like walking on the loose wire.

My father used to give a skunk a quick spray with the hose to send him on his way. Now with the invention of the Super Soaker water gun, a sneak attack on the skunk is possible at all times. A blast to the face is a sure way to get a skunk mad at you, so be careful. For best results, don't let it see where the water is coming from.

Skunks are pretty easy to trap with a live trap baited with cooked bacon. Removing the skunk is another problem, but many animal control agencies will remove the skunk for you.

However, if your local animal control won't help, some local wildlife organizations might. Check with them first. The worse possible scenario is that you will have to remove the skunk yourself. Skunks can carry rabies, so be very careful. Wear gloves and goggles (a skunk's spray can cause temporary blindness). Cut a small slit the size of the trap's handle in a thick tarp. If you are using a Havaheart-style trap that has a handle on top, cut the slit in the middle of the tarp. Holding the tarp in front of you, so you can see through the slit and the skunk can't see you, walk up to the trapped skunk, slowly placing the tarp down on the trap, and aligning the slit with the handle. Let the frightened skunk lie in the dark under the tarp for a few minutes until it calms down. Wrap the tarp around the trap and transport the captured creature off your property. For a safety measure, place the tarp-covered trap in a plastic garbage can with the lid on to keep the skunk's smell out of your car!

A skunk's life

Skunks belong to the family *Mustelidae*, along with weasels, ferrets, and minks. All possess a scent gland, with the skunks possessing the strongest-smelling one. Long ago in Europe, scent glands from animals in this family were used to make a base for perfume.

Four species of skunks are native to North America, with the striped skunk being the most common. They are about 2 feet long, not including the tail, and can weigh up to fourteen pounds (that's one big skunk). Its cousin, the spotted skunk, is much smaller. When threatened, most skunks will stand on their front feet and spray directly over their heads.

Skunks are usually nocturnal and their odor tells everyone that a skunk has been prowling around. Their diet consists mainly of insects and small rodents, and in this regard, skunks are very beneficial. When skunks dig up a lawn or garden, they are usually looking for grubs and other insect goodies, but at times they will eat roots and plants.

Skunks will dig a den in the ground or find a nice spot under a house or patio in which to sleep and have their young. Generally skunks have only one litter of young a year, with the litter averaging five young. The skunk mother will keep the babies with her for the first year.

VOLES

You begin to suspect that mice are running around in your yard in the daytime. They are stripping bark from trees and eating everything in your garden, especially peas and potatoes. However, the culprits are probably voles, not mice.

Sending the vole packing

Most of the deterrents for mice and rats (see pages 12–14) will work for voles. But because voles tend to be active in the daylight hours, you can also set up some predator pest control.

If your yard or property is large, one of the best things you can do is put up a hawk pole. If you've ever visited San Diego's Wild Animal Park, you've probably seen poles about fifteen to twenty feet tall, with perches on top. These poles encourage hawks and owls to come to the area and prey upon the rodent population. If you don't want to erect a new pole in your yard but you do have a large tree, you can remove some of the leaves from one branch to make a good landing area for hawks and owls.

A mouse's cousin

Voles are rodents that can be found throughout North America. They resemble mice, but they're usually brownish-gray, with long fur and short ears. The biggest difference is that voles have tails *shorter* than the length of their bodies. Voles average about 5 inches in length and can produce about four to five litters of five young each per year. One meadow vole in captivity had seventeen litters in one year! That's eighty-five new pests a year from just one mother.

REFERENCES AND BUYING GUIDE

Throughout this book, we've often referred to commercially available beneficial insects. Included below is a short list of some of the commonly requested beneficial organisms. Many more beneficials are available for purchase, and complete lists can be obtained from suppliers, a number of whom are listed in this section.

Some of the beneficial organisms that were mentioned in this book only occur in nature and are not available for sale. For more information concerning the beneficial insects or organisms that would be appropriate and available for your use, contact your local nursery, agricultural extension, or one of the many beneficial insect suppliers who do consulting for the public.

Remember that there may be government restrictions on or permits required for the shipment and release of certain biological control organisms in your state. Before purchasing any organism, consult the supplier or your local agriculture department regarding any restrictions in your area.

COMMONLY PURCHASED PREDATORS AND THEIR PREY

Chrysoperla and *Chrysopa spp.*: green lacewings, a predator of aphids.

Coccinella septempunctata: seven-spotted ladybird beetle, a predator of aphids.

Cotesia melanoscelus: a parasite of gypsy moth larvae.

Cryptolaemus montrouzieri: mealybug destroyer, predator of mealybugs and scales.

Delphastus pusillus: a predator of whiteflies.

Deraeocoris brevis: a true bug, a predator of lygus bugs, whiteflies, pear psylla, aphids, thrips, and loopers.

Encarsia formosa: a parasitic wasp, predator of greenhouse whitefly.

Galendromus occidentalis: predatory mite, predator of western spider mite.

Gambusia affinis: mosquito fish, a predator of mosquitoes.

Heterohabditis bacteriophora: parasitic nematode, predator of mature flies, caterpillars, weevil larvae, and other soil-dwelling insects.

Hippodamia convergens: convergent ladybird beetle, a predator of aphids and for general control.

Orius spp.: minute pirate bugs, predators of aphids.

Podisus maculiventris: spined soldier bug, a predator of gypsy moths and other insects.

Rhyzobius lophanthae: a predator of various scales.

Steninernema carpocapse: parasitic nematode, predator of caterpillars, beetle larvae, and other soil-dwelling insects.

Tenodera aridifolia sinensis: praying mantis, predator for general control.

Trichogramma spp.: parasitic wasps, predators of exposed eggs of various moths and butterflies.

Typholdromus pyri: predatory mite, predator of apple and other orchard mites.

SUPPLIERS OF BENEFICIAL ORGANISMS

The Beneficial Insect Company
244 Forrest Street
Fort Mill, South Carolina 29715
Tel:(803) 547-2301
Retail and wholesale. Catalog. Supplies Southeastern growers.

Beneficial Resources Inc.
P.O. Box 327
Danville, Pennsylvania 17821
Tel: (800) 268-4377   (717) 271-1741   Fax:(717) 271-1187
Retail and wholesale. Exclusive distributor of "Biobest" beneficials and bumblebees.

Bio AG Supply
710 South Columbia
Plainview, Texas 79072
Tel: (800) 746-9900   (806) 293-5861   Fax:(806) 293-0712
Retail and wholesale. Consulting. Food for beneficials. Price list available.

Bio-Agronomics
P.O. Box 1013
Clovis, California 93613
Tel: (209) 297-9288
Retail and wholesale. Consulting services available. Information available on products and services.

Bio-Con Systems
P.O. Box 30186
San Bernardino, California 92413
Tel: (909) 794-5635
Retail and wholesale. Snail control. Free brochure.

Bo-Biotrol, Inc.
9538 Lupin
Winton, California 95388
Tel: (800) 622-9045   (209) 358-1488   Fax:(209) 358-1127
Retail and wholesale. Beneficials, consulting, and products for home and farm. Free catalog.

Buena Biosystems
P.O. Box 4008
Ventura, California 93007
Tel: (805) 525-2525   Fax:(805) 525-6058
Retail and wholesale. International consulting. IPM (Integrated Pest Management) design.

Gardener's Supply Company
128 Intervale Road
Burlington, Vermont 05401
Tel:(802) 863-1700   Fax:(802) 660-4600
Retail and wholesale. Free catalog and gardening consultation.

Gardens Alive!
5100 Schenley Place
Lawrenceburg, Indiana 47025
Tel:(812) 537-8650   Fax:(812) 537-5108
Retail only. Free catalog.

Garden-Ville of Austin
8648 Old Bee Caves Road
Austin, Texas 78735
Tel:(512) 288-6115   Fax:(512) 288-6114
Retail only. Free catalog.

Grangettos Farm and Garden Supply
1105 W. Mission Avenue
Escondido, CA 92025
Tel: (619) 745-4671
Full line of organic products.

The Green Spot
Department of Bio-Ingenuity
93 Priest Road
Barrington, New Hampshire 03825
Tel:(603) 942-8925
Retail and wholesale. Free catalog. Free telephone consultation.

Harmony Farm Supply
P.O. Box 460
Graton, California 95444
Tel:(707) 823-9125   Fax:(707) 823-1734
Retail only. Send $2 for catalog (refunded with first order). Consulting.

Hydro-Gardens, Inc.
P.O. Box 24845
Colorado Springs, Colorado 80936
Tel: (800) 634-6362   (719) 495-2266
Retail and wholesale. Free catalog. Complete greenhouse supplies. Bumblebees.

IFM - Integrated Fertility Mgmt.
333 Ohme Gardens Road
Wenatchee, Washington 98801
Tel: (800) 332-3179   (509) 662-3179
Retail and wholesale. Free catalog. Consulting, tree fruit specialists.

Integrated Pest Management Services
P.O. Box 989
Fresno, California 93714
Tel:(209) 456-0990   Fax:(209) 456-1156
Retail and wholesale.

J & J Aquafarms
P.O. Box 922
Sanger, California 93657
Tel:(209) 875-0477
Retail and wholesale. Aquatic weed and insect control. Mosquito fish.

Mellinger's Inc.
2310 West South Range Road
North Lima, Ohio 44452
Tel: (800) 321-7444 (216) 549-9861
Retail only. Free catalog.

Necessary Trading Company
P.O. Box 603
New Castle, Virginia 24127
Tel:(703) 864-5103
Retail only. Free catalog.

Peaceful Valley Farm Supply
P.O. Box 2209
Grass Valley, California 95945
Tel:(916) 272-4769
Retail only. Free catalog of organic and IPM supplies.

Pest Management Supply, Inc.
311 River Drive
Hadley, Massachusetts 01035
Tel: (800) 272-7672   (413) 549-7246   Fax:(413) 549-3930
Retail and wholesale. Mail order.

Territorial Seed Company
P.O. Box 157
Cottage Grove, Oregon 97424
Tel:(503) 942-9547   Fax:(503) 942-9881
Retail and wholesale. Free catalog.

Tri-Cal Biosystems
P.O. Box 1327
Hollister, California 95024
Tel: (408) 637-0195   (909) 737-6960 in Spanish
Fax:(408) 637-0273
Retail only. Permits for all U.S. states & Mexico

Walter Andersen's Nursery
3642 Enterprise
San Diego, CA 92110-3212
Tel: (619) 224-8271
Full line of organic products. Retail.

Worm's Way Inc.
3151 South Highway 446
Bloomington, Indiana 47401
Tel:(800) 274-9676   Fax:(812) 331-0854
*Retail only. Free color catalog. Organic and hydroponic
gardening supplies, and natural pest controls.*

In Canada:

Bio-Logicals
60 Taggart Court, #1
Guelph, Ontario
Canada, N1H 6H8
Tel: (519) 763-8653   Fax:(519) 763-9103
Retail and wholesale. Permit required for U.S import.

Coast Agri Ltd.
464 Riverside Road South RR#2
Abbotsford, British Columbia
Canada, V2S 4N2
Tel:(604) 853-4836   Fax:(604) 853-8419
Retail and wholesale. IPM consulting. Free catalog. Permit required for U.S. import.

Manbico Biological
Box 17, GRP 242, RR2
Winnipeg, Manitoba
Canada, R3C 2E6
Tel: (800) 665-2494 (Canada only)   Fax:(204) 697-0887
Retail and wholesale. Free catalog. Consulting.

Natural Insect Control
RR#2
Stevensville, Ontario
Canada, L0S 1S0
Tel:(905) 382-2904   Fax:(905) 382-4418
Retail and wholesale. Catalog.

GLOSSARY

abdomen - the posterior portion of the body.

adaptation - any genetically controlled characteristic that helps an animal to survive in its environment.

antenna - sensory appendage located on the head of an insect.

arthropods - invertebrate animals that are members of the phylum Arthropoda, including insects, arachnids, and crustaceans.

bacteria - microscopic organisms that can be parasitic or beneficial, and have round, rod, spiral, or filament-shaped cell bodies.

beak - a protruding mouth part of a sucking insect or bird.

beneficial - a term used to describe a plant or animal that contributes to the well-being of people or nature.

biological control (biocontrol) - the use of organisms or viruses to control or reduce the numbers of parasites, weeds, or other pests.

camouflage - to act or appear like its surroundings, so it can't be seen easily.

carnivore - an organism that feeds on the flesh of other organisms.

caterpillar - the larval form of a butterfly or moth.

chemical control - to reduce the populations of pests by using chemical solutions.

cocoon - a silken case inside which a pupa moth is formed.

cold-blooded - describing an animal that has a body temperature that is regulated by its surroundings instead of its body.

complete metamorphosis - a complete change in form, in the maturing process of certain insects, which involves four stages: egg to larva to pupa to adult.

crawler - the active first stage of a scale insect.

cultural control - to reduce the populations of pests by changing their natural surroundings.

diurnal - describing organisms that are active during the daytime.

entomologist - a person who studies insects.

entomology - the study of insects.

exoskeleton - a skeleton or supporting structure on the outside of the body.

file and scraper - a ridge and angle on the bottom surface of the front wing, near the base, used by crickets to produce sound.

food chain - sequence of how organisms feed on other organisms, including producers (plants), consumers (prey and predators), and decomposers.

frass - termite or wood-boring insect excrement.

fumigate - to use gaseous compounds for the purpose of destroying pests.

grub - the larval form of some beetles.

habitat - a place where an organism normally lives.

hemelytra - front wing of the order of insects called Hemiptera, or true bugs. Means half wing.

herbivore - an animal that eats plants.

hibernation - dormancy during the winter.

honeydew - a sweet liquid that is secreted onto the leaves of plants by aphids and other insects.

incomplete metamorphosis - a change in form during the gradual maturing process from egg to adult in insects. The egg hatches and the tiny insect that hatches looks like a miniature adult. The stages are called molts and there is no pupal form: the insect goes from egg to nymph to adult.

instar - the stage of an insect between successive molts in incomplete metamorphosis.

integrated pest management - a pest management strategy that examines all aspects of pest management and comes up with a comprehensive analysis of the problem, in order to produce the maximum crop yield and the minimum adverse effects to man and the environment.

invertebrates - organisms like insects and worms that do not possess a backbone.

larva - the immature stage between the egg and pupa in insects that undergo complete metamorphosis.

litter - a name given to a group of offspring born to an animal at one time.

maggot - a legless fly larva that does not have a well-developed head.

migrate - to move from one location to another for food or reproduction.

molt - a process of shedding; in insects, a process of shedding the exoskeleton.

negative reinforcement - the act of making something undesirable by associating something negative with it.

nocturnal - describing organisms that are active at night.

nymph - A stage in incomplete metamorphosis. Nymphs are immature insects that resemble tiny adults. Several molts may occur during this stage.

omnivore - an organism that feeds on both plants and flesh.

ootheca - the covering or case of an egg mass.

order - a subdivision of a class of organisms, containing a group of related families.

overwinter - the ability to spend or survive the winter.

parasite - an animal that lives in or on the body of another living animal (the host) for at least part of its life. This parasite animal may or may not kill its host animal.

parthenogenesis - the production of offspring without fertilization.

pest - an organism (either plant or animal) that is harmful or annoying to humans.

pheromone - a substance produced by one organism that influences the behavior or physiology of another organism of the same species.

predator - an animal that attacks and feeds on other animals (prey).

proboscis - an extended mouthpart, which in insects can be beak-like or tube-like.

pupa - the stage between the larva and the adult form in insects with complete metamorphosis. This stage is nonfeeding and inactive.

quarantine - to reduce the number of pests by isolating and excluding them from certain areas.

queen - a female that is capable of reproduction in a colony of social insects.

scavenger - an animal that feeds on dead plants or animals, decaying materials, or animal wastes.

scientific name - an internationally recognized Latinized name for a species.

skeletonize - to reduce something, such as a leaf, to skeleton form.

species - a group of individuals that are similar in structure and physiology and are capable of reproducing fertile offspring.

suborder - a major subdivision of an order, containing a group of related families.

thorax - the body region in insects between the head and the abdomen, which has the walking legs and wings.

torpor - a form of dormancy that is used by animals such as hummingbirds to conserve energy.

vector - a transmitter of disease or pathogens.

warm-blooded - describing an animal that has its body temperature regulated from within its body.

wildfly - a term to describe a fertile, non-irradiated fly.

BIBLIOGRAPHY

Borror, Donald J. and Dwight M. DeLong. *An Introduction to the Study of Insects*, 3rd ed. New York: Holt, Rinehart and Winston, 1971.

Burt, William H. and Richard P. Grossenheider. *A Field Guide to the Mammals of America North of Mexico*. Boston: Houghton Mifflin Company, 1976.

Dadant & Sons. *The Hive and the Honey Bee*. Carthage, IL: Journal Printing Company, 1975.

Debach, Paul. *Biological Control by Natural Enemies*. New York: Cambridge University Press, 1979.

Fichter, George S. *Insect Pests*. New York: Golden Press, 1966.

Flint, Mary Louise. *Pests of the Garden and Small Farm*. Oakland, CA: Division of Agriculture and Natural Resources, University of California, 1990.

Gay, Kathlyn. *Cleaning Nature Naturally*. New York: Walker and Company, 1991.

Grainger, Janette and Connie Moore. *Natural Insect Repellents*. Austin, TX: The Herb Bar, 1991.

Kerr Kitchen. *Pantry*. Los Angeles: Consumer Products Division of Kerr Group, Inc., 1995.

Kilgore, Wendell W. and Richard L Doutt. *Pest Control: Biological, Physical, and Selected Chemical Methods*. New York: Academic Press, Inc., 1967.

Marer, Patrick J. *The Safe and Effective Use of Pesticides*. Oakland, CA: Division of Agriculture and Natural Resources, University of California, 1988.

Metcalf, C. L. and W.P. Flint. *Destructive and Useful Insects*. New York: McGraw-Hill Book Company, 1962.

Orr, Robert T. *Vertebrate Biology*. Philadelphia, PA.: W.B. Saunders Company, 1971.

Pleasant, Barbara. *The Gardener's Bug Book*. Pownal, VT: Storey Publishing, 1994.

Pringle, Laurence. *Pests and People*. New York: Macmillan Publishing Co., Inc., 1972.

Routhier, William. *Africanized Honey Bee Reference Manual*. San Diego, CA: California Department of Food and Agriculture, 1994.

Garden Pests & Diseases. Menlo Park, CA: Sunset Publishing Co., 1993.

Tyrrell, Ester Quesada. *Hummingbirds, Their Life and Behavior*. New York: Crown Publishers, Inc., 1985.

Unitt, Philip. *The Birds of San Diego County*. San Diego, CA: San Diego Society of Natural History, 1984.

INDEX